Volume III

HIS

MYSTERIOUS

WAYS

Volume III

HIS

MYSTERIOUS

WAYS

The Editors of Guideposts

Guideposts Associates
Carmel, New York 10512

His Mysterious Ways, Volume III

All Scripture quotations, unless otherwise noted, are from the King James or Authorized Version of the Bible.

Scripture quotations marked RSV are from the Revised Standard Version of the Bible, copyright 1946, 1952, 1971 by the Division of Christian Education of the National Council of the Churches of Christ in the United States of America and are used by permission.

Scripture quotations marked NIV are from the New International Version of the Bible, copyright © 1978 by New York International Bible Society, and are used by permission.

Scripture quotations marked CEV are from *The Bible for Today's Family,* Contemporary English Version, copyright © American Bible Society, 1991, and are used by permission.

Every attempt has been made to credit the sources of copyright material used in this book. If any such acknowledgment has been inadvertently omitted or miscredited, receipt of such information would be appreciated.

Except as noted below, and for some poems, all material appeared originally in *Guideposts* magazine. Copyright © 1953, 1959, 1960, 1963, 1966, 1972, 1975, 1976, 1977, 1978, 1980, 1981, 1982, 1983, 1986, 1987, 1988, 1989, 1990, 1991, 1992.

"A Strange Soft Light," by Malcolm Muggeridge is from *Something Beautiful for God,* by Malcolm Muggeridge, copyright © The Mother Teresa Committee, 1971, and is reprinted by permission of HarperCollins.

"A Friend Was in Danger," by Margaret Mackay, is condensed from the book *I Live in a Suitcase,* by Margaret Mackay, published 1953 by The John Day Co.

Arthur Gordon, "Seconds Away from Death," and Carol Knapp, "The Afterthought," are from *Daily Guideposts 1992,* copyright © 1991 by Guideposts Associates, Carmel, NY 10512, and are used by permission.

Don Bell, "The Steer in the Soaphole," is from *Daily Guideposts 1989,* copyright © 1988 by Guideposts Associates, Inc., Carmel, NY 10512, and is used by permission.

The poem "When" by Sallie Chesham is from *Wind Chimes* by Sallie Chesham, copyright © 1983 by The Salvation Army, and is used by permission.

The poem "Promise" by Sallie Chesham is from *Catalogue Roses* by Sallie Chesham, copyright © 1987 by The Salvation Army, and is used by permission.

The poem "God Fashioned a House," is from Grace Livingston Hill, *The Parkerstown Delegate.*

Book design by R studio T
Cover art by Mike Jaworski illustrates the story on pages 47–48.
Printed in the United States of America.

CONTENTS

PREFACE

*M*y cousin Anna was not—"relatively" speaking—a close cousin, but we were very close. I say this in spite of the fact that in the years after my tenth birthday I lived in New York and she in Kentucky. We only saw each other maybe once a year and neither of us kept in touch with letters. Anna must have been in her late forties by the time I came into my teens, though I never thought much about the difference in our ages. We were friends. Soul mates, you might say.

One night during my junior year of high school I put away my homework, turned out the light, and slipped into bed. But I did not go to sleep. I began to think about Anna. The clock ticked. Sleep would not come. *Anna. Anna.* She simply would not leave my thoughts. Finally I got up out of bed, turned on the light, sat down at the desk and wrote her a letter. She never received it. That was the night Anna died.

Her death shook me, yet shocked and saddened as I was, what really unnerved me was how Anna had come so insistently to mind as I struggled for sleep that night. It made me feel odd. Had I dreamed it all? No, the letter was proof that something real had happened between Anna and me. Even so, it gave me such a strange feeling that I was reluctant to tell anybody about it. Today, however, I no longer try to fathom the mystery of that night. I simply accept it gratefully as a beautiful spiritual confirmation of how close Anna and I were to each other.

Back then I had no way of knowing that other people had similar mystical experiences they couldn't explain. Now, after many years as Editor-in-Chief of *Guideposts* magazine, I know that these things happen all the time. Again and again readers of the magazine have written to tell us of the strange happenings in their lives. The book you hold in your hands at this moment is filled with such accounts. As you read them may I suggest that you do as I did and not struggle for explanations. Stand in awe if you will, but be grateful for their mystery. See them as a wonderful confirmation of God's presence in our lives.

VAN VARNER
Editorial Director

PART ONE

How
God
Works

One

THAT
STRANGE
INNER
URGE

*J*esus left Judea and started for Galilee again. This time he **had** to go through Samaria, and on his way he came to the town of Sychar . . . [where] a Samaritan woman came to draw water from the well.
—John 4:3–5, 7, CEV (emphasis added)

The inner nudges that cause us to change direction, to stop or to keep moving when common sense and circumstances tell us to do just the opposite, and that end up saving lives or putting us in the right place at the right time, are hard to explain apart from God's mysterious workings. We see them at work in Jesus' life. And when we heed them, we become partners in God's work in the world.

The Premonition
J. V. Calvert

What is it, Lord? What's this weird feeling that something unpleasant is waiting for me down the road?

As usual, I was talking to my Friend as I drove through the muggy August night at 3:00 A.M., hauling forty-eight thousand pounds of steel in my eighteen-wheel rig.

I knew nothing mechanical was wrong. As careful truckers do, I'd done a thorough job of checking everything before leaving on this round trip run between Fort Worth and Bryan, Texas. The only thing I'd found to worry me was a creepy spider skittering across the dashboard. I'm six feet two and fifty-two years old, but I'm a baby about spiders. Using my leather driving gloves, I'd brushed it out of the cab.

But now this strange sixth sense was telling me that I ought to be extra careful, extra wide-awake. I'd never had it before, and I kept trying to turn it over to the Lord:

Lord God, You're my Father, and I know You want what's best for all Your children. So now I ask You to ride this run with me—sit real close, keep me alert, help me get rid of this crazy feeling that's bugging me. I give You the honor and the glory . . .

A lot of truckers are big on CB radio talk for passing the time. I'd rather talk to the Lord. I had grown up in a family where talking to Him and singing His praises were as natural as breathing. So on these long, dark, lonesome runs I make for

Central Freight Lines, it is second nature for me to ask Him to keep me company. Each night I always pray and sing the old familiar hymns. Doing that helps me feel ready for any surprises that might come my way. But this night I couldn't seem to relax.

By 6:45 A.M. I'd picked up my return load of forty-three thousand pounds of bleach and was on my way back to Fort Worth. I planned to make my usual breakfast stop at the Dixie Cafe. But when I got there and parked—do you know that sneaky uneasiness wouldn't let me go in? *Don't stop now,* came the urging. *Keep on moving down the road.*

I sat still a few seconds, trying to resist it, thinking about juice and eggs and coffee. Then my hand reached for the ignition switch.

With something like a groan, I began to ease the rig out of the parking lot. *J. V.,* I told myself, *you can handle a truck just fine, but this fool thing going on in your head is something else.* And then: *Please, Lord, I'm counting on You to stay here in this cab with me.*

Out on Highway 6, I concentrated on the road. Only two lanes wide, it didn't give a tractor trailer much room for maneuvering. Unconsciously, I began to sing again: "Jesus loves me, this I know, For the Bible tells me so . . ." I hadn't sung *that* since I was a little kid.

About thirty miles from Waco, I glanced in my side-view mirror and saw a trucker coming up fast on my tail. He was in an empty truck or he wouldn't have been able to highball it like that. Since I was hauling a slow, heavy load, I pulled over to let the empty truck overtake me. As the driver whizzed by, he raised his hand in the traditional signal that says, "Thanks, good buddy." Soon he was three hundred yards down the road.

And then it happened. Sitting high in my cab, thirteen feet off the ground, I had a bird's-eye view of the trucker's nightmare unfolding in front of me. In a flash, something had made that big rig go out of control. It reeled across the wrong side of Highway 6 and careened along the shoulder. Then, in a slight incline about seventy-five yards off the highway, it flipped over, jackknifed, and turned bottom-side up. I heard a monstrous *vroom*, as if a giant match had been struck. Fire and black smoke mushroomed from the cab area.

I'd already stopped my rig a safe distance away. Now I raced down the highway, my knees pumping like pistons. *O Lord, have mercy,* I prayed as I charged toward the fiery cab.

When I came around the truck and saw the driver, I thought he was a goner. His bleeding head and shoulders were wedged in the broken window behind the steel supporting braces of the big side mirror. The braces were bent so they formed prison bars, and the bottom of the mirror was embedded deep in the ground.

O Lord, have mercy! Give me the power to yank that stuff loose! Just then, the man moaned and I knew he was alive. I took a deep breath, grabbed the mess of steel braces and half-buried mirror, and jerked it with all my strength. Unbelievably, the whole thing broke free!

Please, God, don't let him be stuck in that flaming cab.

"You're gonna have to try and help me, buddy," I pleaded. The trucker's arms were pinned to his side, but he began to move.

"That's it! Keep wiggling!" I pulled and eased him out of the cab window frame onto the ground.

O God, let us get away from this truck before its gas tanks explode.

I helped the man up, and he began stumbling up the incline on his own. But he was in shock—covered with blood, dirt, and shattered glass—and he collapsed on the grass almost immediately. We *had* to get further away.

It was then I looked up, because something very unusual was going on. The wind was out of the south, more than just a breeze. Fire and smoke should have been billowing in our direction. In fact, the wind should have blown fire and smoke directly on me as I was dragging the driver out of his burning cab. But it hadn't. Instead, I could see the smoke swirling straight up, arching over the truck—over us—and coming down in the middle of the highway like a rainbow. How long could it last?

Frantically I helped the man get up again. Just as we reached a safe distance about fifty yards away, the gas tanks blew, incinerating the tractor trailer as if it were just a wad of dry paper. And at that same instant, the smoke and fire began blowing the way they should have all along—igniting the area we had left only seconds before.

Thank You, Almighty Lord!

Suddenly people began appearing out of nowhere, beating out the grass fire and then gathering around us—another truck driver, motorists who'd stopped. In the distance I could hear an ambulance siren.

Someone showed up with a first aid kit. Other people started picking glass out of the man's shredded shirt and cleaning him up. The ambulance arrived. So did the Highway Patrol and a local fire department. My job was done.

As I was walking toward my truck, a bystander caught up with me. "Hey, you saved that man's life! No one else had the guts to go near that truck—scared it would blow any second."

I shook my head. "I don't want the credit," I told him. "I just try to stay close in touch with the Lord. So when I need help, He's there to give it. *He* gave me the push and the strength and a couple of miracles this morning, and He gets the glory."

I thought for a minute and then I started to chuckle. "You think I've got guts? Why, man, you're looking at a guy who's scared of a little spider!"

WHEN
Sallie Chesham

Courage has no banners,
Courage has no drums,
But softly, when the heart asks God,
Courage always comes.

In triumph.

SECONDS AWAY FROM DEATH
Arthur Gordon

*W*hen I was a college youngster I was much interested in crew racing. Mostly I rowed in an eight-oared shell that competed in various regattas. Now and then I would also try rowing alone in a single scull, a fragile splinter about twelve feet long, barely a foot wide, very light, very fast and very unstable—any awkward or sudden movement could easily tip it over.

On this weekend our crew was competing at a college where the rowing took place on a broad smooth river. In our practice outing we had rowed upstream from the boathouse, as did the other crews, not downstream. But I gave no particular thought to this.

Early in the morning, with time to kill, I went down to the boathouse and took out a single scull. It was a beautiful day, sunny and warm. For a change of scenery I decided to row downstream. In a single scull, unless you turn your head, you can't see where you're going; you guide yourself by watching the shoreline as it slides past. With the current and a breeze aiding me, I seemed to fly across the burnished water. In almost no time I had covered a mile, keeping to the middle of the river with no thought of danger.

But suddenly something made me look over my shoulder, and when I did my heart seemed to stop. Fifty yards farther on *the river disappeared.* It simply vanished, because it was pouring over a dam or breakwater at least twenty feet high. Now I could hear the muffled roar it made as it plunged into the gorge below. In that terrifying moment, I knew that I was only seconds away from death. I stopped rowing and sat there, frozen, but the current carried me on.

To turn a single scull you back with one oar and pull with the other, but gently, gently, not too hard. You're supposed to take your time, but I had no time. Two words flashed through my mind: *Don't panic.* To this day I don't know how I did it, but I whirled the scull around, hooked the racing water with both blades, drove my shoulders back and my legs down, and felt the scull leap like a waterbug away from the dam and back upstream into safety.

Just lucky? Too many questions remain. What made me look around just in time? Why did I *not* panic? How did I manage to spin the scull around, keep my balance, and start moving back upstream? Today, more than half a century later, the old familiar phrase still echoes in my mind. Just six words: *But for the grace of God. . . .*

THE STRIP MINER
Bill Carver

I was barely out of my teens when our weekly paper in Greenville, Kentucky, began running stories about the great new shovel Peabody Coal was putting together at their mine in the low hills just outside of town. Whenever I could, I'd ask for time off from my stockroom job and drive out to watch.

I could hardly believe the size of the machine that was taking shape out there. Her crawlers went up first, so big they dwarfed the buses that brought the welders out to work on her. Her housing went up next, and then came the boom carrying the stick and bucket that would strip away the hills from the miles-long, six-foot-thick seam of coal that lay beneath the surface. That bucket was the size of the living room in the new home my bride, Dorothy, and I had. No wonder the crews that would operate No. 3850 were already calling their shovel "Big Hog."

Then came the day in March 1962 when I joined a small crowd of men to watch the huge yellow-and-green shovel fire up for the first time.

"You could stand the Statue of Liberty under that boom," said a voice behind me, "and still have ninety feet to spare."

I turned and saw a neighbor who worked at another mine.

"Someday," I told him, "I'm going to run that shovel."

"Not me," the miner said with a laugh. There was an approving murmur from other men standing around. The problem, it seemed, was responsibility. The mine and the

TVA power plant that made electricity from her coal would employ four hundred men. To keep them busy Big Hog had to operate twenty-four hours a day every day of the year. If that shovel stopped working, everybody stopped working. "I'll take a little less money and sleep nights, Bill," the miner said and turned to walk away.

But responsibility was something my daddy had raised me to live with. It was my job as a boy to chop kindling and milk the cow morning and night. Once, I didn't get my work done. That day my father came in from the underground mine where he worked and took me aside and told me that when I had a job to do I was expected to do it. Always. No questions. We depended on each other, my father said, and that was a good and a God-given thing. So men depending on one another didn't stop me and Dorothy from praying that someday I'd be up there in that glassed-in operator's cab.

At last when I was twenty-nine years old and three of our four children had already been born, a position on the shovel did open up. Midnight, April 14, 1969, I stepped onto the company bus with the rest of the hoot-owl shift. It was a mile trip now, across the plain Big Hog had been making out of the Kentucky hills, to the place where the shovel was sitting on the seam of coal she was uncovering. The bus stopped beside Big Hog, and we got out and stood in the floodlights and noise beside the crawlers.

"Well, Carver," shouted the shift operator, "there she is—Big Hog."

He nodded us toward the elevator, and moments later we were standing in the housing just outside the operations cab, a hundred feet above the pit floor. Big Hog's generators whined and her winches screamed, but to me the noise sounded great. We stepped into the cab and shut the door, and at last you could hear! The cab was spotless, just as I thought it would be, a bright yellow and green, with a lot of glass above and around us. The first thing that struck me was the great speed. The operator turned his housing back and forth on its rollers like a man running a whirl ride at an amusement park.

I was introduced around, and the men seemed glad to have me aboard, as if they sensed I was part of the breed that would like it up there. My job was the lowest on the four-man crew—mostly it was cleaning and moving things, but it was a way to get ahead.

I spent the first three years learning the ways of Big Hog, moving slowly up the ranks. One of my chores as oiler was to scramble up the boom to its highest point. Not everybody would like riding point. Those days, they didn't stop the shovel while you climbed the boom's ladderlike steps. The boom danced up and down, swiveling left and right at a dizzying speed. If Big Hog hung her bucket into hard rock while you were up on point, she shuddered and bucked, and you'd better grab onto something if you didn't want to fall two hundred fifty feet.

I tried to ride point just at dawn so I could see the sun come up. What a place for my own kind of quiet time, sitting on the very highest part of the shovel with nothing above me but just heaven. Peabody prided itself on putting the land back the way it was, minus the coal. They saved the topsoil we dug and then spread it on the worked-over land and replanted it. Wildlife was already coming back. I'd wait up there on point, watching as the deer came down to drink at the new lake. Muskrats and coons and possums and foxes and a raft of geese were out too. That was my time for thinking what an amazing thing it was for God to give us this place to manage.

The company encouraged operators to train crewmen on the controls, because on-the-job was the only way anyone could learn. One night after I'd been on Big Hog a little over three years I came in for coffee and stood behind the operator. Then came the question I'd been waiting for.

"Want to see what she feels like, Bill?"

Did I! The operator showed me what I already knew: which lever moved the housing, which moved the boom, which lowered or raised the stick and bucket. He showed me the emergency Kill Button that would shut the shovel down dead. "Hope you never have to use *that*," he said.

The operator stood up and I took his place, and then I barely touched the lever that moves the stick toward the highwall. I was astonished. It was not at all like the work I had done on a bulldozer. Big Hog's living-room-sized bucket moved with no more effort than it takes to throw a light switch.

"Different from a dozer, isn't it?" the operator said.

Different, yes, but not easy. Your bucket was half a football field away from you. You had to time yourself just right or you'd scramble thousands of dollars worth of cables. Each move had to be precise. You just eased that bucket up, shearing off the dirt and rock.

Years went by and I liked my work more as each day passed, especially when I was up on point, knowing Dorothy was home praying for us. Dorothy kept a CB radio scanner by our bedside, tuned to the company channel which off and on through the night would crackle with talk between the shovel and the office. When the radio woke her up she would pray for us.

Which is the only way I can explain what happened the morning of the accident.

I'd finally made it to the top. Our operator had been letting me take longer and longer turns at the controls, and when he retired, after I'd been working on Big Hog for eight years, I was next in line for the job. Everything went smoothly at first. But then came the night of March 4, 1980.

Fifteen minutes before quitting time it was still dark outside. Three of us were in the cab; our oiler was off somewhere. How can I understand what happened then? Something was *wrong* with Big Hog. I heard inside my head the idea, *The bucket's going to break in two.*

I whirled around.

"Get down!" I shouted. I hit the Kill Button.

Big Hog stopped. The men backed away from me, puzzled, because nothing seemed wrong out there in the night.

At that instant there was a sharp report, like shot going off at the highwall. I watched dumbfounded as the bottom of the bucket fell off. Tons of dirt and rock hit the pit floor. Dust flew up in the floodlights. The stick snapped its cables. Exploding sounds cracked all around as the arm-sized cables broke and lashed our cab and wrapped around the boom. Rivets popped like machine guns going off. "This is it!" someone whispered. Through the dust cloud I saw the great boom buckle, crumble, fall almost in slow motion to the floor of the pit. Rocks. Smoke. Screaming metal.

And then silence.

I looked around the cab, covered with shattered glass. The two men with me in the cab were shaking but safe. Where was the oiler? "Richard!" I shouted. We pulled and yanked and pried at the wedged door until at last it gave . . . and there stood Richard in the ruined housing just outside the cab. Stunned, safe.

I got home hours after the ambulances came racing into the pit. Now I was sitting at our kitchen table with Dorothy, neither of us talking much. It wasn't until I tried to tell her about the strange warning that I knew how strung out I was. The warning had given me only a few seconds, but without it I wouldn't have hit the Kill Button *ahead* of time. We'd still have been under power and those cables would have just kept on hitting us. As it was, no one was hurt.

No one, that is, but Big Hog.

There in our kitchen my mind went back to the shovel lying in her own wreckage on the floor of the pit. Suddenly my lip began to tremble. I looked at Dorothy and we both knew I was going to cry. I put my head down on the kitchen table, not ashamed to weep, and Dorothy didn't stop me.

At first I didn't want to go out to the mine to see Big Hog stretched out. But then Peabody announced that they had made a decision. They'd rebuild No. 3850 if it took every welder in the United States. Sure enough, three months after the accident I climbed into the operator's chair again and looked through the floodlights toward the highwall. I touched the starter. Big Hog fired up smooth as could be, and once more we began making coal.

One thing about any mine: sooner or later the seam itself runs out. We worked for four more years but then reports began to filter through that the coal was pinching off. We knew our jobs would be finished soon, and one day the superintendent himself came in.

"Boys," he said, "it's been a good mine, but we're about through."

And so we were. I'll never forget the day, fifteen years after I first went to work on the shovel, when I got into the elevator for the last time, climbed onto the company bus, and rode away.

And Big Hog? It was impractical to walk her to another mine, too expensive to cut her up and move her elsewhere. So they took our shovel to the middle of the pit and there they made her dig her own grave. When she couldn't go any deeper they brought in a drag line to finish the job.

For weeks I refused to go out to watch or even to think much about Big Hog. What was over was over.

But then I got to thinking. Soon 3850 would be gone. Maybe I could do something to keep her *memory* alive. Which is why I'm putting this down now, so my grandchildren will know what kind of work we did at the mine.

I don't think I'll end with the account of the burial, though. Instead I'll talk about the morning when I was back up in the cab for the first time after the accident. The shift was coming to a close that morning, and it was the hour I used to have by myself up on point. I couldn't go up there much anymore. But that morning from my operator's chair in the cab I spotted a deer on the highwall, and I recalled all those dawns when I used to watch the wild animals break cover.

For a quarter century here at our mine, human beings and

wild creatures and hard black coal had come together, and it all took place around Big Hog. You can't watch that without something happening to you. That's what I want to say to my grandchildren. I want to tell them how it is that a man and a coal shovel can have something between them that goes . . . well . . . beyond just having a job to do.

WHEN THE BELL TOLLED
Judy A. Armstrong

Mrs. Webb was blind and frail and her health had been declining for many months. She and her husband lived in the shadow of our church, First Baptist, in Headland, Alabama.

On New Year's Eve she went to bed early as usual while Mr. Webb watched TV. Then unexpectedly at 10:30, she came into the living room and announced, "Honey, I think we should stay up until midnight and hear the church bells ring."

In all the years they had lived in town, Mr. Webb could not remember hearing church bells at midnight on New Year's Eve. As far as he could recall, the bell at First Baptist had not been rung in over seventeen years. Nevertheless Mr. Webb replied, "Of course, dear, come and sit beside me. We'll see the new year in together."

And so they sat and talked, waiting. Midnight came and

with it the unmistakable sound of a church bell. "There it is," Mrs. Webb said, and, indeed, the bell high in the steeple at First Baptist was ringing.

That was to be the last night that this old married couple was to spend together, for in the morning Mrs. Webb died peacefully in her sleep.

Mr. Webb did not know that the bell at First Baptist had only recently been fixed. Nor did he know that a youth group was spending the night in the church in a "lock in," or that on the spur of the moment the young people would decide to ring in the New Year. His wife knew none of these things either, but she knew the bell would toll.

The Gideon Bible
Marion Bond West

*W*hen I married Gene after both our spouses had died, what I wanted most was to be a good minister's wife. His first wife, Phyllis, had been perfect at the task.

For twenty-five years she'd been a church organist, organized women's groups, taught Bible classes, sang, counseled, planned church socials, was a marvelous cook. She was always patient, loving, supportive, loyal. She even invited the entire congregation to their home for fellowship.

My biggest challenge came when Gene took an interim

pastorate in Perry, Oklahoma. As we drove there, I struggled with unspoken feelings of deep inadequacy.

That summer morning we were leaving a motel in Jackson, Tennessee, after visiting family in Georgia. Gene was preoccupied with loading the car and planning our day's drive. I picked up the Gideon Bible as I waited for him and prayed for guidance.

"Let's go," Gene finally announced, bags in hand. I started to replace the Bible on the table, then received an unmistakable urge: *Leave it on the unmade bed—open.* I'd never done such a thing before. Yet somehow it felt right, almost familiar.

I left the motel room ahead of Gene, with some hand luggage. When Gene joined me, I was startled to see tears in his eyes. He was so moved he couldn't speak. We both sat silent in the car for a moment, then he said, "That's something Phyllis did in every motel we ever stayed in, a witness to whoever cleaned the room."

As we headed west on Interstate 40, I felt just a little bit like a minister's wife.

"SHE KNEW YOU WERE COMING"
Fred Nicholas

On Christmas Day a young man, tall and slim with dark hair, was making his way south on Interstate 85 just below High Point, North Carolina, trying to hitch a ride.

For two years he hadn't been home; his family had heard nothing from him. He and his mother had had a disagreement, and he set off across the country, going from town to town, from odd job to odd job. He worked at filling stations and produce markets; he drove a taxi and picked crops; he was an orderly in a nursing home and a plumber's assistant. But now he was ready to go home.

Thirty miles to go, but a ride was hard to find. "Mom," he said to himself, "I'm tired and hungry, but I'm coming home."

The cold wind blew and a few trucks rumbled by. Then from across the road, he heard a voice call his name. "Mike! Hey, Mike, come here!" To his surprise there was his stepfather, waving, calling to him from his truck. Mike ran across the highway. "Get in, Son. We're going home."

Mike tossed his bag in the back of the truck and embraced his stepfather. "Fred," he said, "how did you happen to be here?"

"I came to pick you up," Fred said to his own amazement. "Drove straight here."

"But how did you know I'd be here? I didn't write. I didn't call."

"Your mother sent me. Just this morning in her prayers for you, she *knew* you were coming and that you were on Interstate 85 just below High Point."

The two men looked at each other without saying a word. Then Fred started the motor. "She's waiting for you, Son."

Two

THOSE

INEXPLICABLE

EVENTS

*W*e found the prison securely locked and the sentries standing at the doors, but when we opened it we found no one inside [the prison]."

—Acts 5:23, RSV

Sometimes wonderful things happen to us for which we can find no logical explanation—except God's intervention. We receive needed information in mysterious ways or are miraculously saved from sure distruction without doing anything ourselves. Unopened letter bombs, steers who get out of deadly bogs by themselves, and Bibles that tell their owners when it's time to be passed on to someone else are some of the inexplicable events in this section that demonstrate God's care for all His creation.

What Stopped the Tractor?
Alan Holland

Seven years ago I had a stroke that left me paralyzed on my right side. Back home on our farm I learned how to walk again, how to write, even how to drive our tractor. I could control its throttle with my left hand, the brakes with my good foot, and turn the steering wheel with one arm.

And then one day something went awry. While mowing the grass, I hit a concrete block. The left wheel jumped, and I was knocked out of the driver's seat, my right foot caught between the brake pedals and my body dangling over the side. On and on the tractor went, my head bouncing six inches above the mower's whirling blades.

"Mike, Mike," I screamed for my son. The tractor was heading for a barbed wire fence. I'd either be crushed under the tires, or the wires would rip through me. But suddenly the motor stopped. The wheels and blade stopped moving. My paralyzed leg relaxed and I gently fell to the ground.

I lay there stunned. Why had the tractor stopped? It was in gear, the gas was locked in full-throttle, the tank was full. My son and mother came to help me into the house. "What stalled the engine?" I stammered. They dressed my wounds, and my neighbors came to see if I was all right. "I'm fine," I replied, "but what stopped the tractor?"

Someone said it might have been the grass, someone else suggested a faulty ignition wire. "Go look for yourself," I said. There was no grass clogging the mower blade. And as for the ignition, they could see for themselves.

I was saved fourteen years ago; when that tractor started up on the first try, I knew He was still my Saviour . . . and now my savior.

THE UNOPENED PACKAGE
Lynn Grisard Fullman

On a Saturday in December 1989, a Birmingham federal judge was killed by a letter bomb mailed to his home.

On Sunday Willye Dennis, head of the Jacksonville, Florida, chapter of the NAACP, was scheduled to attend a press conference. However, she arranged to have the meeting postponed until Monday. She wanted to attend a Sunday memorial service for two victims of another bombing—one that had happened twelve years earlier.

On Monday a package was delivered to Willye Dennis's office. She was busy that morning and didn't have time to finish opening her mail before leaving for the press conference.

After the press conference, Willye was heading back to the office when her car broke down. The engine ran but the wheels wouldn't move. Two police officers tried but couldn't make the car budge. A wrecker was summoned but it stalled.

A second wrecker was called but it failed. Finally Willye rented a car and drove home.

On Tuesday morning, before dawn, Willye received two calls at home. A friend phoned to tell her about a letter bomb that had killed a civil-rights attorney in Savannah, Georgia. A little later her niece called for their morning prayer time. Only then did Willye think of the brown paper package on her desk at work. Later that day she alerted the sheriff's office. It was discovered that the package contained a bomb. A bomb meant for her.

All of this causes Willye Dennis to say today, "God is alive. The Lord will have His way and no human being can stop it."

A Dog Named Bandit

Ronald "Scotty" Bourne

For a number of years I have been placing a little figure of a dog next to the infant Jesus in my Nativity set at Christmas. Some people raise their eyebrows, but when they hear my story, they feel differently. For it represents a real dog, named Bandit. Whether he belongs there, you judge for yourself.

I got Bandit in 1967 when I was working as an animal trainer for Walt Disney Productions. We were filming *Three Without Fear,* a TV movie about three children and a dog trekking across a desert. We needed an animal that looked like a starved Mexican street dog.

At an animal shelter in Glendale, I found a part German shepherd. His ribs protruding through his mangy black-and-gray fur, he fit the part. Bandit was what local children had called him for stealing food.

Bandit turned out to be a natural actor. He took direction well and was always ready to play. Sometimes the play got out of hand. When we were filming near Scammon's Lagoon in Mexico, someone threw a stick into the ocean for him to retrieve. A strong undertow carried him along the shore. As he struggled to keep his nose above water, I raced along the high sandbank, trying to reach him before he was carried out to sea. At the last second, I managed to grab his collar and pull him to safety.

Another time, in Arizona, a little raccoonlike animal called a coatimundi, which was appearing in a scene with him, bit Bandit's leg. The animal's razor-sharp teeth severed an artery, and two crew members and I made a mad dash by car sixty miles across the desert to a Tucson veterinarian. As I held Bandit in my arms, I realized how much my friend meant to me. Thank God, a fine vet helped pull Bandit through. I decided then it was time he retired from the movies.

For a while Bandit lived with my sister's family in Simi Valley. He thrived on domestic life and became a neighborhood hero. As his movies appeared on television, there was a constant demand for him to "speak," "shake hands," and pose for pictures. Bandit loved the attention and had infinite patience.

Moreover, he had an almost human understanding of people's needs. For example, one of my sister's boys was born with splayed feet. The doctor prescribed braces and told her not to expect the child to walk at the normal time. However, one day to everyone's surprise, Bandit was seen walking very slowly across the yard with the baby toddling behind, hanging on to the dog's bushy tail!

Then came a time when everything in my life fell apart. After a broken romance, I was at my lowest ebb. Bandit and

I got back together again, and during long reflective walks on the beach, he was my only companion. Though now graying at his muzzle, he still wanted me to throw a ball and play with him. This was my therapy, for Bandit coaxed me out of my melancholy solitude.

As my outlook improved, I deepened my relationship with the Lord. This led me into many new areas, one of which was a juvenile prison ministry. Bandit accompanied me on my visits to the teenage boys; they loved to hear his story, especially about my finding him in "prison."

However, by 1979 Bandit was old and painfully stiff; I sensed it would be his last Christmas, and I asked the Lord to help me make it especially significant, not only because of Bandit, but because of my new life with God.

By mid-December I was afraid Bandit would not even make it to Christmas. One day while praying over him, I envisioned myself going to the stable at Bethlehem. Carrying my old friend in my arms, I presented him to the infant Jesus. I explained to Jesus that my gift was the only treasure I had left. Slowly, I placed Bandit beside the baby Jesus, then turned and walked away.

The picture I had while praying became a reality on Christmas Eve. Bandit lay on the lawn, unable to stand. His brown eyes, glazed with pain, looked up at me imploringly. In anguish I called the animal shelter, and I placed Bandit in my car for the last time. The man at the shelter took him gently, and I stood waiting outside until he brought me Bandit's collar; he put his hand on my shoulder and told me it was all over.

All the way home I begged, "Lord, I know he was just a dog, but he meant the world to me and I loved him. Please let me know if he is with You."

I was still grieving the next morning as I arrived at the detention camp to conduct a Christmas communion service. I really didn't feel like being there. The boys were at a low point too, for they had nothing to give their families, who would be visiting later in the day. Our service was held in a small television room, the only decoration being a simple Nativity set on the table which served as an altar.

As I talked to the boys about the spirit of giving, I said, "People place too much emphasis on expensive gifts. The greatest gift you can give is what you seem to place the least value on. While we're taking communion, I suggest each of you offer Jesus the one precious gift that no one else can give: yourself."

When it was over, as the boys started filing out the door, I happened to look down at the manger scene. I stared transfixed. Standing beside the crib of the baby Jesus was a little statue of a dog. A dog that looked like Bandit—in the exact spot where I had placed him in my prayer.

With a tight throat I asked, "Who—where did the dog come from?" The boys all shook their heads.

No one at the center had any idea who put the small figure of a dog there or where it came from. So I gently put the figure in my pocket, looked up, and silently thanked God for answering my prayer.

And that's why I have a little dog next to the baby Jesus in my crèche.

THE STEER IN THE SOAPHOLE
Don Bell

I've heard it said that God keeps His eye on the sparrow. I think He keeps it on all His creatures, sometimes in ways that are hard to understand.

Back in 1958, I was a range cowboy looking after a bunch

of steers for a man by the name of Smoky Grabbert, who ranched in Emblem, Wyoming. I had moved three hundred head of Angus steers to Dry Creek for summer pasture. Later I would have to move them to the mountains, so one day I rode through the Pitchfork Ranch Range country getting acquainted with the land so I would know the shortest way.

As I rode alone through this big country, I noticed a two-year-old Hereford steer stuck in a quicksand hole. Pitchfork Range had many of these dangerous holes; we called them soapholes. Today these holes are fenced, but back then they were open. This steer had stopped struggling, so I roped his head and tried to pull him out, but my horse was not stout enough to move this eight-hundred-pound critter.

I rode back to camp to get a four-wheel-drive pickup, chains, shovel, and a hoist. I drove back at breakneck speed, because I knew the steer would soon sink and die. Lo and behold, as I approached I saw the steer standing on dry land some distance from the soaphole. Perfectly safe!

To this day I don't know how that steer got out. I asked every Pitchfork cowboy and no one had even been in that area. It made me realize that I wasn't the only one looking over that steer. Someone with much more power than I had taken care of that animal. His eye was on the sparrow, and it was on that steer too.

Those Mysterious Numbers
Edith M. Dean

*M*y husband, Jim, and I were getting ready for bed when the phone rang. The stranger explained she was Grace Morrison's aunt, "calling from Nebraska," and Grace's brother had been seriously injured in a car accident. No one knew how to get in touch with Grace. Did I?

Grace and I had once been office friends, but we hadn't spoken in years.

"I'm sorry," I said after fumbling through my Rolodex, "I don't have Grace's address or phone number. Let me call you back if I find it."

"No, I'll call you in the morning," the woman said.

The memory of that pleading voice kept me up for hours looking through old files and address books. When I went to bed, I prayed and then tossed and turned, thinking of phone numbers in my sleep. When I woke up in the morning my favorite ballpoint pen was lying on the nightstand. I had no idea how it got there.

I left early for work that morning, but when I came home Jim exclaimed, "Thanks to you, Grace Morrison is on her way to Nebraska."

"Thanks to me?"

Jim looked at me, puzzled. "Yes. When her aunt called, I gave her the number you had written on that pad on the nightstand. Then she called back to say all was well."

"But, Jim," I said, "I never found it."

"Look," he said, handing me the pad. There in my handwriting was the correct phone number for Grace Morrison.

I sat down, mystified. And only then did I wonder: How did the aunt find me?

THE PASS-ME-ON BIBLE
Fred Nicholas

During a low point in my life, I was at a yard sale and came across an old, well-thumbed Bible. "How much?" I asked the woman presiding over the table.

She looked at me searchingly, and then surprised me by saying, "If you promise to read it, I'd like to give it to you for free."

I accepted both the Bible and the challenge. True to my promise, I read that Bible again and again, and as I did, things seemed to turn up for me. Eventually I bought myself a new Bible, and a day or so later when I picked up the old one, something strange happened. It was as though a jolt of electricity passed through my hands. The old book seemed to say, "Pass me on."

A few days later I was talking to a man who was deeply troubled. I told him he needed the kind of help to be found in the Bible. Since he did not own one, I offered him mine.

A year later I met the man again, but he was happier, more confident, and he told me that the old Bible had changed his life. "But I don't have it anymore," he said.

"Why?" I asked.

"Well," he said, "it looked so shabby I bought myself another one to carry to church." And then he looked at me quizzically, as though he wanted to say more.

"Yes?" I asked.

"You won't believe this, but one day I was dusting my bedside table after I bought the new Bible, and when my hand touched the old book, I felt a surge of electricity pass through me and—"

"The Bible spoke to you!" I exclaimed.

"Yes. 'Pass me on,' it said."

DEEP IN GOD'S WILDERNESS
Doug Elliott

T here is a sacredness in nature. Perhaps you feel it too. Nature has molded me and taught me, and it is deep in the heart of the woods that I feel happiest, and closest to a spiritual presence, closest to God.

The story I'm going to tell you is about a time when I experienced that mystical presence. It came in an unusual way, and it taught me the importance of being still, of listening.

At the time I didn't know what to do with my life, how I would make my living. I had a degree in art from the

University of Maryland, and yet, with all of that education, I didn't want a regular nine-to-five job. Like many young people out of school, I wondered, *What now?*

I had no job offers and no idea of what to do with my degree. I'd grown up in the Chesapeake Bay community of Severna Park, Maryland, in the fifties and sixties. Now, in the early seventies it was time to fill some purpose, time to earn my way.

Growing up had been the same for me as for most kids in our area. Scouting, public school, supportive parents, and Sunday church had helped in the making of me. The only difference, I suppose, was that I seemed much closer to nature. Dad always said, "Doug knows what's under every rock between here and town," and that seemed fine with my folks. No one ever disapproved of my backyard menagerie or yelled at me when a frog was seen hopping across my room. They listened faithfully to the nature "lectures" I gave to Cub Scouts and to classes.

For a time after finishing school I dabbled with paints and did landscapes and abstracts at my grandmother's farm in New Hampshire. But that was a tough way to make a living. I grew restless. I wanted to see the rest of the country, and one spring day I stuck out my thumb and headed down the road.

I traveled through New York, then southwest across the Appalachian Mountains down to Memphis and the banks of the Mississippi. I took a factory job, briefly, then headed on through Arkansas and Oklahoma and across the top of Texas. And everywhere I went the same question traveled with me: *What will I do with my life?*

It followed me across the Rio Grande and into the Indian town of Gallup, New Mexico, where I hopped a freight for California and watched landscapes to the rhythm of the wheels.

Clickety-clack, clickety-clack through the mesas, where Navajo women herded sheep. *Clickety-clack, clickety-clack* through Arizona's desert painted by sunset. *Clickety-clack, clickety-clack* into the cold of the night. *Clickety-clack, clickety-clack—what will I do? What will I do?*

After a number of weeks along the Pacific Coast I made my way north, up to British Columbia and the edge of the Rockies, where one morning I was hitchhiking along the New Denver Road. I hadn't seen a sign of civilization for miles. I was wondering if a car would ever come along. Finally a young couple stopped to give me a lift, and after an exchange of introductions and a few miles of getting acquainted they invited me to camp with them.

"What do you do?" they wanted to know.

"Well, that's a question," I told them. "I studied art in school, and now I'm traveling around the country to see what I can see."

There was that question again. People everywhere wanted to know *what do you do?*

We stayed by the stream that followed the road. We fished and shared our food. I showed them how to find stinging nettles and to steam them like spinach. But we didn't talk much. They were quiet, and that wound me down. I began to listen, carefully. To sounds around me. To feelings inside of me.

The peaks of the mountains loomed overhead, and I felt an urge to climb to the top. To stand at the top and to look out and to feel that mixture of elation and humility. To be one with nature.

I told my friends that I'd be back by nightfall, packed a lunch, my sketch pad and pen, and waded across the stream toward the slope. A dipper bird fished upstream from me, and on the other bank a couple of large toads sprang out of my path. There was no trail. I had to bushwhack my way up the mountain, through brush and forests. All morning I climbed up, and up, and up.

It was hard work, and in the heat of the climb I peeled off my sweater. It was spring in the Rockies, early June, and young leaves were just beginning to open on the lower side of the mountain.

Despite the upward struggle, the fallen trees and thickets, the tricky footings, I felt exhilarated by the challenge and by the anticipation of reaching the peak. There would be something special there. A view. A feeling. Something, I felt.

Breaking a wad of spruce gum from a tree trunk, I chewed it on the trek up. I scrambled higher, higher, through the spruces, until, finally, I reached a high rocky ridge.

Oh my! I'll never make that peak, I realized. It was far in the distance, magnificent, covered in snow. I could never reach the top and return to camp by nightfall. *I'll have to turn back,* I thought, disappointed.

I sat on a ledge and ate my lunch, and thought to myself that few people had ever reached this perch or looked out at this majestic wilderness. Maybe none. I felt that I could see forever, over miles and miles and miles of God's creation. And in the quietness of that spot, I opened myself to the beauty around me.

I listened. And I sketched the panorama of peaks; then I started back.

And that is when it happened.

I was going down, down, back into the timber, pushing my way quietly into a thick growth of spruce trees, when I was startled by a sudden *whir-r-r-r* of wings.

I'd flushed a bird, a large one. But instead of flying off, it landed on a branch hardly ten feet away!

It looked like a partridge, with red wattles on each side of its beak. Its feathers were mottled brown, except for its tail, which was chestnut-tipped.

I later identified it in a guidebook as a bird rarely seen because of its wilderness habitat. It was a spruce grouse.

"How strange," I muttered to myself. I felt almost in awe of this bird. But what struck me as particularly eerie was this—the bird almost seemed to be *talking* to me!

Ko-o-o-ok, ko-o-o-ok, ko-o-o-ok. It stared at me and made that soft sound. Very quietly.

I waited, spellbound, for it to fly from the branch. But it didn't. It stayed and kept looking at me and uttering, *Ko-o-o-ok, ko-o-o-ok, ko-o-o-ok.*

I watched for several minutes. Then I eased out my sketch-book and started to sketch him. And he remained.

I'd never known a bird to act like that. It was as if he wanted to be near me. Quickly I drew a rough sketch, hoping that he'd stay. He just perched there curiously bobbing his head, watching me sketch, and uttering, *Ko-o-o-ok, ko-o-o-ok, ko-o-o-ok.*

I made another sketch, and another with a few more details. I felt myself caught up in the excitement of drawing this strange and beautiful bird. Excited by the discovery. Excited? Thrilled!

I felt a thrill. *This is it! This is it!* My mind seemed to explode with the discovery, with the relief of knowing.

"Here I am high in the Canadian Rockies drawing pictures of rugged wilderness landscapes and unusual wildlife, combining my love of the outdoors with my years of training in art school. I'm a *wildlife artist!*" This seemed like the fulfillment of a lifelong dream. "A wildlife artist!" I could hardly contain myself.

"Here I am on my own, drawing this bird. Nobody hired me. No museum sent me. I came here on my own, and I can develop a career on my own—combining nature and art. It is possible! I'm doing it now, and I can do it for the rest of my life."

And that's what I've done. I wrote and illustrated a book entitled *Roots,* an underground botany and forager's guide. I've taught people how to weave fibers from wild plants, how to make baskets from bark, how to make silk from cocoons. I've lectured at the Museum of Natural History and I've taught at the Smithsonian Institution.

The spruce grouse, the bird that started me on my way,

flew out of my memory until a year or two ago, when an Indian friend brought him back to mind.

"I'll bet I know a bird you've never seen," he challenged me.

"Which one?" I asked.

"The spruce grouse. A bird that lives in the far north," he said.

"I did see a spruce grouse once," I told him, "in the Canadian Rockies. He made a strange little sound like this: *ko-o-o-ok, ko-o-o-ok, ko-o-o-ok.*"

"Do you know what the Indians say about him?"

"No," I replied. "What?"

"We call him the messenger bird. He often brings an important message."

I stood speechless, thinking back to that grouse staring down at me, repeating over and over his message. A message that had shaped my life.

And now, in nature, I try to listen more closely, with my whole spirit. And it is in nature that I feel most aware of the spiritual messages that I need to hear. Listen carefully. You might hear them, too.

THE YELLOW ROSE
Charlotte Doty

November 3 was my birthday. As I drove down the mountainside to Holy Apostles Episcopal Church in Hilo that Sunday morning, I couldn't help but miss Mother. It had been six months since her death, and this would be the first birthday I had to celebrate without her, without the cake she always baked, or the table she always decorated with yellow roses. Our family had lived in Hawaii for fifty years, but Texas-born Mother was always "The Yellow Rose of Texas," her house filled with that mainland flower.

At church I slipped into the pew. "I miss Mother so," I sort of prayed, kneeling with my head in my hands. I couldn't bring myself to look at the flower-filled urns on their tall koa-wood stands. The brilliant orchids and anthuriums could only clash with my gray mood inside.

The first hymn brought me unwillingly to my feet. That was when I saw it, not on the stands where flowers were always placed, but right on the altar: a tiny bud vase.

And in the vase a single yellow rose.

It was the best birthday gift I could have received, this reminder that those we love are never far away.

At the service's close, I hurried to the Flower Guild chairman to find out who had left this bud on the altar, a place I had never seen flowers before. But she was as puzzled as I and told me that the vase didn't even belong to the church. And though we queried every guild member, and anyone else who might have brought flowers, no one could explain how the rose came to be there.

To this day I don't know how—only Who.

Three

THE

MYSTERIOUS

VOICE

*T*hen a voice came from heaven. . . .

—*John 12:28,* RSV

God's messages sometimes come in an audible voice—but from "nowhere" that we can see or explain. Often at the time we don't realize that the message is from Him. At other times we know that the voice is God's. The question becomes, then, whether we'll obey. When we do, we discover more of God's mysterious and wonderful ways.

PILOT'S DIRECTIONS

David Moore

Henry Gardner was flying me to Asheville, North Carolina, in his Cessna 180. We'd taken off from Victoria, Texas, and stopped in Jackson, Mississippi, to fix a malfunctioning radio. Now we were nearing Asheville only to find that the fog was so thick that the controller wouldn't let us land. "Sorry," he said over the radio, "you'd better head to Greenville."

But we couldn't. We didn't have enough fuel to make it there. "We're going to have to land," Henry insisted. We were granted permission to make an emergency landing. The radio sputtered a few times and he lowered the plane.

"Pull it up!" came the shout. To our horror we saw we were about to land on the interstate! Henry pulled hard on the stick and we barely missed a highway overpass.

"If you listen to me," the voice on the radio said, "I'll show you how to get back in." And then came a series of careful, detailed instructions: "Raise it up." "To your left a little." "Easy, easy." "You're nearing the runway. Let it down—now!"

Suddenly the lights of the runway appeared out of the fog. Never had I seen such a welcome sight. We landed safely. First we thanked God. Then as soon as we could, we went to thank the air traffic controller, who looked at us in bewilderment.

"I don't understand," he said. "I lost contact with you after I told you to make an emergency landing. Your radio sputtered and you were gone."

THE VOICE OUT OF NOWHERE
Robert Meeler

I was thirty-eight when the Lord spoke to me—and told me to do the strangest thing.

We had a little farm in the mountains of north Georgia then—me, my wife Nell and our six children. I'd never been to school a day in my life and I couldn't read a word, but I did know how to farm. I'd learned that from my father. The day I heard God speak was a beautiful one, the kind where the sun blazes down and warms your bones. I was bending over, picking a mess of peas for supper, when out of the blue a Voice boomed: "I WANT YOU TO GO PREACH!"

I jerked up and looked around. *Some rascals are playing a trick on me,* I thought. I ran to the big rock on top of the hill, where I could see for miles. But when I got there, not a soul was in sight—and not a sound could be heard except the birds' chirping and the soft swish of the wind. I was sure then that God Himself had given me an order, and I began to shiver. Why would He want me, an ignorant farmer?

"No, Lord!" I cried into the sky. "I can't preach. Not a man like me with no learning. Why, I can't read Your Word. Besides, I'm too new a Christian."

A couple of weeks before, Nell had taken me to a prayer meeting, and that night I'd accepted Christ. But how could a brand new Christian preach to others?

"Don't *ask* me, God," I mumbled, looking down at my cracked, dusty old brogans. Then I started to run down the hill, away from that Voice.

As it turned out, I kept right on running for five years, because during that time I didn't go to church much. I didn't have time for it. A farmer leads a busy life, seven days a week. Or so I told myself.

Those were lean, hard years for our family. Everything seemed to go wrong. My crops failed, I was in a bad accident with my pickup truck, and—worst of all—my sweet little daughter Betty died with infantile paralysis. I walked around half-dazed most of the time and that got me into more trouble.

Where I lived, getting ready for planting meant burning off the fields before plowing. I knew perfectly well how to burn safely, but the spring that Betty died I wasn't paying full mind to the job. I raked brush into a pile to start the fire, and when I bent down and struck the match, I didn't notice the wind had picked up.

All at once the wind whooshed across the field and whipped my fire out of control. I *had* to keep it away from the sprouting fields my neighbor had recently planted! I panicked—raced into the fire and tried to beat it out. Instantly I was completely surrounded by flames. They roared higher than my head, and right then and there I thought about the gates of hell. "Lord, save me!" I yelled. "I don't want to die. Save me, and I'll do what You want!" The last thing I remember is covering my eyes with my arm and dashing through a wall of fire.

I was badly burned and spent a long time in the hospital, but God answered my prayer. Now I had a promise to keep—somehow. I had to find a way to do what He wanted.

Shortly after I was on my feet again I sold my hard-luck farm and moved my family to what I hoped was a better one near Lyerly, Georgia. Now every Sunday, without fail, I went with my family to the Belmont Baptist Church. I had a lot of catching up to do.

Several years passed and I did my best to honor God and learn about His teachings. Just by listening hard, I memorized a good amount of Scripture. I wasn't preaching, but I was never shy about testifying for the Lord. Then one day the church deacons called me aside.

"Bob," they said, "we'd like you to teach the adult Sunday school class."

"I can't," I told them. "I don't know how to read."

But those people were a good bunch of friends. "That doesn't matter, Bob," they said. "You'll make a good teacher anyhow." They wouldn't let up urging and encouraging me.

I was still ashamed about my ignorance, but I remembered my promise to God. *Maybe this is what God meant when He told me "go preach," I thought. Teaching is almost like preaching. Maybe this is what He had in mind all along.*

I accepted the job.

Before each class my wife, bless her, read the lessons to me. I couldn't have done the job without her. But Nell didn't have much formal schooling and there were many words she couldn't make out herself. After two years, I began to feel frustrated. I needed to learn to read for myself. Even with a lot of back-patting from the folks in my Sunday school class, I felt they deserved a lot more than they were getting from me.

If only I could get some schooling . . . but we were still poor. And even if I could afford to take time away from my farm work, how could a codger in his fifties fit into a classroom with little kiddies? Impossible! The blues began to gather around me like clouds around a mountaintop.

One day, fed up with the daily torment, I decided to *will* myself to read. I grabbed my Bible and stomped into the woods behind our house. I sank down under a pine tree and opened the Good Book. The mass of black letters all seemed a jumble. None of those little marks printed on the page had any meaning to me. I tried so hard to make them out that my head began to hurt and my stomach knotted up. Tears welled up in my eyes, and I slammed the book shut and let them come. Inside me there was a deep ache, and it came out in great moans.

"Lord," I sobbed, "You know my misery. You *know* I'm trying to serve You. I want to do what You want me to do, but I don't know how. I need to read Your Word, but I can't. Dear God, help me!"

For hours I sat there, crying and begging for help from above. At last a peaceful feeling settled over me. I didn't know what it meant, but I felt better, as if Someone had put a hand on my shoulder and said, "It'll be all right now."

That night, I was listening as Nell read the Bible to me. She stumbled on a word, and without thinking I leaned over to look at the page. "That's 'impoverished,' " I said.

She picked up reading where she'd left off until another word stopped her. Again I looked at the page. "That's 'inhabitants.' "

The third time it happened, Nell got a funny expression on her face. "You know this Book better than I do," she said.

And all of a sudden it hit me. *She was reading verses I hadn't memorized!*

Almost fearfully, I took the Bible from her and ran my eyes over the page. "I can read, Nell," I cried. "I CAN READ!"

I flipped page after page and every sentence made sense. I even picked up a magazine and read the words on the cover. "It's got to be God's work," I whispered. "Only God could do this for me."

How long had He been planting His words in me so that now, this night, they had sprouted and bloomed? Without another word, we got down on our knees and gave thanks to Him.

I stayed up late that night, searching the Scriptures with my own eyes. What a joy to read for the first time the words in Job 32:8, "It is the spirit in a man, the breath of the Almighty, that makes him understand" (RSV).

To me, those words will always have a special meaning.

They say that every one of us has a secret Teacher who lives within us. If you ask His help—and trust in His wisdom—you'll be given whatever knowledge you need to have.

How else could an ignorant old farmer learn to read without ever setting foot in a schoolhouse?

Editor's note: Robert Meeler, who was eighty-three in 1982, when this story was published, taught his Sunday school class for seven more years. Then he became the preacher for a church in Alabama, finally fulfilling his promise to God.

SOMEONE'S KIDDING!
Kennith Bishop

*B*ack in the mid-fifties, when I was out of the Army and uncertain about my direction in life, I got a job at Superior Marking Products in Chicago, a company that made ink, type, type trays, date stamps, toy printing presses—anything that had to do with printing. I operated a vacuum press and enjoyed it, and I enjoyed my fellow workers. Especially Joe.

Joe was a big, burly man with a deep faith. He'd been at Superior for almost thirty years and commanded a lot of respect. Whenever he talked, we listened. But I never listened more closely than during an afternoon coffee break when he told us about something that had happened to him years before, right there in our company warehouse.

Joe had been in the warehouse, working. He was alone. When the time came to leave, he turned out the lights and headed for the freight elevator. He could hear his own footsteps echo in the silence as he walked down the dark aisles. He was about to step into the freight elevator when he heard, "Joe, Joe."

Someone was calling his name. He turned and looked around, but he could see no one. "Who's there?" he called out.

No answer.

Someone's kidding me, Joe thought. He called out again, but still there was no answer. He shrugged and turned again to the elevator, but this time he stopped.

Before him were the open doors of the elevator shaft, but no elevator, only a long, long drop into nothingness.

WARNING AT 5:12
Elva and Ben-David Weisiger

ELVA WEISIGER'S STORY

The sound of quail calls and the tinkle of goat bells made the peacefulness of the Southern California mountains seem especially beautiful that late afternoon. It had been another lonely day, but I didn't mind living on the isolated ranch. It had been our family home for over thirty years. My nineteen-year-old son, Ben-

David, and I were all who were left on the place. That summer, however, he worked for the Division of Forestry in the mountains and only returned home on weekends.

While standing at the sink peeling a potato for my supper, I looked up from the damp brown and white strips to the clock mounted on the wall in front of me. The time was twelve minutes past five.

Suddenly, from nowhere, a voice said, "Pray. You must pray!" The potato thumped into the sink. In stunned amazement I whirled, knowing no one would be there. Yet I had clearly heard a voice.

Again it commanded, "Pray! You must pray!"

Shocked surprise shook me to my heels. Fear gripped me by the throat. Tears washed down my face. I felt some calamity was about to happen. Forcing down sobs, I closed my eyes, "Dear Heavenly Father, please help . . . !" *Pray for what? Pray for whom? Why?* But the voice said, "Pray!"

Completely puzzled I began again, "Dear Heavenly Father, please take care of whatever I am supposed to be praying for. You told me to pray, but I don't know why. I'm putting it in Your hands, Lord. Please take care of whatever needs help."

I stood praying until a feeling came that some crisis was over. But apprehension clung to me like a wet coat as I went about the evening chores. My mind filled with tortured thoughts as the mountains took on the rose-colored glow of sunset. Could one of my sisters be in trouble, or Ben-David? I had no phone, so all I could do was wait.

BEN-DAVID'S STORY

Five o'clock, quitting time! I sighed with relief, for the job of installing pipe corrals for the Laguna State Park Horse Heaven was heavy and tiring. It would be good to get back to the place where I boarded for a shower and dinner. The pine trees smelled spicy in the late afternoon heat when I drove the old Chevy down the winding road at my usual pace. On the back seat was a heavy automotive part that needed repairs.

With no warning at all the right rear tire blew out. As I fought against the heavy pull on the steering wheel I felt the rivets on the right front wheel shear off. For the only time in my life I lost control of my car. It flipped over. In one terrifying moment I looked straight down at the black-topped road. All I could think of was the automobile engine head that I had laid on the back seat. It bounced around like a cardboard box. As the car rolled over and landed on its wheels, that heavy metal casting hurtled toward me. Horrified, I pushed hard against the door trying to get away from it. The door sprang open, throwing me unhurt to the ground just as that head crashed through the window where I had been!

I got to my feet thoroughly shaken. I kept thinking, *I could have been killed. Only a miracle saved me from death!*

A wrecking truck from a nearby village drove by a short time later. He towed the car to the house where I boarded. There I called a friend to come take me home.

Twilight shadows filled our valley when we got there. Mom met me at the gate. She looked strained and concerned. "Are you all right?" she asked. She grew pale as I told her about my accident.

"When did it happen?"

I thought back. "I quit work at five, so it must have been between 5:10 and 5:15. Mom, I was really shook! The Good Lord was with me that time!"

"God was with me, too," she said with her voice choked with emotion. Then she told me about the voice she heard and the strong premonition of danger.

Did her prayer help save my life? I'm sure it did. How comforting to know that even today, He still cares and watches over us.

The Long Leap
Jose M. Sandoval

*F*ifty years of traveling around the world as a U.S. merchant marine should be enough adventure for anyone. But not until I was an old man living alone in New York City did I experience the most terrifying night of my life.

I was living in a little room in a men's hotel on 34th Street. Recently released from a veterans' hospital after four months of treatment, I was blind in one eye, with only partial vision in the other. I was worried. How would I get along? I had always been an independent person. But now, to be almost blind? Still, I was grateful to be back on my own and, with a cane, could get around somewhat.

One March night in 1972 I went down to the street for a paper and chatted a bit with the news vendor. As I headed back to the lobby, I could just about see the neon cross of the mission down the street glowing through the mist. It made me feel good. As the elevator took me to the seventh floor where my room was, I thought back on how God had helped me through my seventy-two years. As a young soldier in Guatemala, about to drown in a raging river, I turned to Him, and the torrent swept me to safety. Some years later I was aboard a ship wallowing helplessly in a hurricane. Again, He was there.

As I settled in bed, I offered my nightly prayer. "O Father, thank You for this room. Thank You for still being able to read the paper." I relaxed and then fell into a sound sleep.

Dimly, I heard shouting. *It's probably some young men quarreling in the alley,* I thought. I turned over. But the noise increased. Then I began to hear bells, like fire bells. I crawled out of bed, fumbling for my glasses. I checked my watch; it was nearly eleven o'clock. I picked up the phone to call the desk and find out what was going on. No answer. I jiggled the hook, but the phone was dead. Apprehension began to build in me. This was an unfamiliar building; I didn't know my way around it. Now I could hear sirens wailing from far below.

Fire? Could the building be on fire? I had to find out.

I opened the door to the hall and fell back as thick black smoke billowed into the room. I slammed the door.

"O God, I've got to get out of here!"

I remembered a metal fire-escape door down the hall. I pulled on my pants, donned a raincoat, hat and winter gloves, then wrapped a wet towel around my face. I could hold my breath for two minutes. Within that time, I knew, I had to get out that fire door.

When I pulled open my door again, thick, hot, asphyxiating smoke swallowed me. I groped along the walls, sensing through my gloves the paint bubbling on the plaster, hearing the crackle of flames, feeling the searing heat.

Ah, the fire door! I grabbed the hot metal handle and pulled. Nothing. It was swollen tight into its frame by the heat! I yanked at it. Now my lungs were bursting. "Don't breathe!" my mind screamed. But I couldn't hold my breath anymore. My chest surged as I gasped for air.

There was no air—only a hot, swirling pitch that burned my nostrils, choked me, filled me with sickness. My legs crumpled and I seemed to be dizzily whirling into a black vortex, dimmer, dimmer. . . .

And then I seemed to hear a voice, strong, powerful, commanding: "Run to the window! Fast! Run!"

It shocked me. And then, perhaps from years of instantly obeying commands at sea, I rose and began running blindly, twisting, turning through the labyrinth of corridors.

And then I saw it. A dim light. I rushed to it and found myself in front of a small window. I lifted it. Surprisingly it slid up easily, unlike the usual paint-sealed windows of old buildings. I leaned out, gasping, filling my lungs with fresh, cold air.

As my head cleared, I looked down to the street at the end of the alley far below. It was alive with the activity of fire pumpers and the clamor of the crowd. In the garish brilliance of floodlights, tiny faces looked up to the front of the building. Would anyone see me there at the side in the dark?

I leaned farther out the window. Behind me the inferno roared as timbers exploded into flames and walls buckled and cracked. Now heat seared my back. My coat began to smolder.

I had to get out.

In the dark, about six feet from the window, was a large round chimney pipe. But I saw no hope of a handhold on its wide sooty girth.

But wait. What was that? Farther down an iron brace-bar extended from the chimney to the building wall. It looked much too far for me to reach, but in desperation I reached for it anyway.

I remember nothing more until I found myself clinging to the brace. "Thank You, Lord," I breathed, as I got a firmer grip. I looked down to the street. No one could possibly see me up here.

Then I remembered the little flashlight I always carry in my coat. Anchoring myself with one arm, I carefully reached into my pocket. I waved the flashlight. No one seemed to notice. About ten minutes passed. I rested. Fifteen minutes. I began to tire. Twenty minutes. My body ached in the cold night air. Slowly I waved my flashlight. Still no one seemed to notice. Twenty-five minutes. My muscles cramped and I began to shake in pain. I looked at my hand; it was white from clutching the bar. Was it a part of me anymore? I wasn't sure.

Below me infinity stretched seven stories to the concrete

pavement. As I feebly swung the light, an insidious feeling came over me. How relaxing it would be just to let go, just rest my tired muscles. And then I remembered. God had brought me this far. I could not let down now. I waved the flashlight again.

A thin cry floated up: "Don't jump!" Had someone seen me? And then other voices rose, encouraging voices: "Don't jump." "We're coming . . . hold on!"

New strength flowed through me. I felt I had won a battle with something far darker than the smoke pouring out of the window above me.

And now I was bathed in light. As the fire ladder reached toward me, I could hear cheers from the street. The ladder halted just below me, trembling as a fireman scrambled up. "Here," he called. "I'll help you down."

"No, thank you," I said as my feet felt for the step. "I can make it." *An old man can still have dignity,* I thought, as I eased down the ladder to safety.

The next day a TV cameraman and I walked through the charred halls to the window I had escaped from. He looked down at the iron brace and whistled. "That's quite a distance. How did you do it?"

So I told him. I told him God had shown me the way to that window and that I was sure He had helped me reach that brace.

He stared at me for a moment, then turned to set up his equipment. Whether he believed me is something I don't know. But I do know without a doubt that I couldn't possibly have escaped that burning building without God's help.

I know too that I don't have to worry anymore about how I will get along with my limited eyesight. The Lord has shown me that He will always be with me.

BACK OFF!
DeLinda Koster

I drummed my index fingers on the steering wheel as a big, dusty tractor-trailer rig lumbered in front of us on the curvy two-lane country highway. *If we can get around this poky truck,* I thought, nudging the accelerator and peeking out into the other lane, *we can make up some of the time we lost.*

Mom and I, on a visit to Missouri for a Mother's Day family reunion, had planned to spend the morning with my grandmother—Mom's mom—at the nursing home, then join the reunion. We were anxious to visit with Grandma; because of her age, we did not know if we would ever see her again. But it had been one thing after another this sunny Mother's Day. We'd been late getting on the road, then traffic had been snarled by a nasty pileup. Now it was this slow-motion truck.

I glanced over at Mom. Her face was a mask, but she wrung her hands in her lap. I knew how much she wanted to spend time with her mother. *I've got to get around this big old truck,* I thought.

As we came out of a turn I eased the car over the center-line. There was a short straightaway before the next curve. Normally I don't pass, but no cars were coming from the other direction and I thought I had enough time to scoot around the tractor-trailer. Then, just as I tramped the accelerator into passing gear, I distinctly heard a voice warn, "Back off!"

Startled, I immediately let up on the gas and swerved back

to my lane. I checked the rearview mirror. Nothing. I shot Mom a quick look. She seemed oblivious. Hadn't she heard that?

As we headed into the next curve I dropped back from the truck. I hadn't been aware of following too close. *Not that it matters,* I complained silently. *This guy's not even going the speed limit!* Nevertheless, I fell back a little more and tried to distract myself by glancing at the greening countryside flashing by. I cracked the window a bit to suck the stirring smells of spring into the car. Pieces of my rural Missouri childhood seemed to rush in on the fresh wind. This was such a familiar stretch of road, Highway 13 heading toward Osceola. I used to lie on my back in these fields and gaze into the clear blue midwestern sky, searching for airplanes. I'd imagine that a plane would fall from the sky and I would have to pull the injured aviator from the wreckage and save his life. Funny. How many times I'd had that Florence Nightingale fantasy!

I turned to Mom. "It's nice to be back," I said, speaking quietly because I knew how jumbled her emotions were. She looked at me and with a sigh smiled for the first time that day. A verse from Philippians popped into my head: "And the peace of God, which passeth all understanding, shall keep your hearts and minds through Christ Jesus."

I noticed I was back on the tail of the diesel rig. *I've got to get around him.* I checked traffic. All clear. I flipped on my turn indicator and glided over into the opposite lane. And then I heard it, the same warning voice, this time even more distinctly: "Back off!"

I jerked the car back behind the truck. *This is really strange,* I thought. I looked at Mom. She fiddled nervously with a bag that contained some things for Grandma, but still didn't act as if she'd heard anything. I peered at the truck. It didn't look out of the ordinary.

All I could think about was getting past this truck, putting it as far behind us as possible. Smoke belched from its exhaust pipe as the driver wheezed through the gears on a hill. I glanced at the dashboard clock. We were really running late. As we hit another straight stretch of road I gunned the engine. As I nosed the front of the car even with the back of the rig, the voice came again: *"I said back off!"*

Now I really was scared. I jerked the car back into our lane and leaned hard on the brakes. Turning to Mom, who was staring at me with a startled look, I began shakily, "I don't think you've noticed, but the oddest thing has—"

Suddenly my mother pointed straight ahead. "Dear God, DeLinda, look out!"

In a flash of dust and gravel the big truck swerved, buckled and with a terrifying screeching of brakes slammed into a pickup truck pulling a camp trailer. I frantically veered onto the narrow shoulder, sliding to a stop just yards from the tractor-trailer rig, which stood upright but jackknifed at an angle that seemed to defy gravity.

Mom and I leaped out. Diesel fuel fumes and the odor of hot rubber hung in the still air. Mom raced to check on the drivers and passengers. A hundred yards or so off the road was a tiny country store. Crunching across the gravel and through high dry grass in my high heels, I made a stumbling beeline for it. "Call an ambulance right now!" I cried to the owner. "There's been a smashup!" Then I dashed back to the crash.

"Folks in the pickup are okay," Mom reported, "just a little shook up." Then she pointed up to a burly, motionless figure slumped over the steering wheel in the truck cab. "I can't rouse him, though."

Cars were pulling off the road and a small crowd began to gather. The stench of diesel fuel was getting thicker. Suddenly someone pointed and shouted, "Look out!"

A lake of fuel was spreading rapidly on the road from a rupture in the truck's gas tank. People began to back away. Then I noticed the sound: The truck's engine was running! Mom kept yelling up at the cab, "Mister, can you hear me? Mister, wake up! Mister!"

"Mom, we've got to get that engine shut down before

there's an explosion." Suddenly I was scrambling up the side of the tall, tilted truck cab. It was wedged at such a precarious angle that I wasn't sure it wouldn't roll over and tumble into the roadside ditch. When I neared the cab window I bellowed at the driver, "Wake up! Shut it off!" He was breathing but blood was gushing from a nasty gash between his eyes. "Sir! *Shut it down!*"

He stirred. He moaned. He tried to raise himself up but slumped again against the wheel. The fumes were getting stronger.

"Stay awake!" I screamed. "You've got to turn the engine off!" I could not reach the ignition myself; I was barely hanging on to the outside of the cab.

"Can't . . . do . . . it," he stammered.

"You've got to," I said, "or it'll explode." With all my might I prayed, *Lord, give this man strength.* Slowly the man's fingers moved, then his hand, then his arm inched forward. Below me Mom was pleading, "Hurry, DeLinda!"

With a trembling hand the driver reached out. His fingers found the ignition and with a terrible gasp he twisted the key. The engine stopped.

"Good work," I said. "Now we've got to get you out of here. There's gas everywhere." I tried to open the door but it was hopelessly jammed. "Roll down your window!" I called. He grimaced and shook his head. "You can do it," I said. Agonizingly he inched down the window as far as it would go.

Now what? I wondered. The driver looked at me helplessly. He was exhausted. There was no way someone of my size could lift this big man out of the window of the truck. But I had to do *something.*

"Sir, put your hands on my shoulders. Lean your weight on me and I'll climb down the cab with you." I looked down at Mom. If I could support the man for just a few feet, Mom could reach up and help.

He put all his weight on me. My heel slipped. I clung to

the cab for dear life and took another step. My knees buckled but I held on. The driver was groaning as he slipped through the window. My hands trembled, my knuckles went white. Then I felt Mom's hands holding me up. Together we pulled the man from the wreckage and dragged him away from the truck. In the distance came the wail of approaching sirens.

"Are they okay?" he asked, meaning the people in the pickup. "Are they alive?"

"Don't speak," Mom hushed him. "Those folks are just fine. You're the one who needs tending to."

We kept the driver awake but quiet until the paramedics arrived. We didn't want him losing consciousness and going into shock. When the attendants loaded him onto a stretcher I noticed the trucker still had his driver's log at his side. Attached to it was a picture of his young son. "You stay awake until they get you to the hospital," I said. "That little boy needs his father."

Then Mom and I were back on the road toward the nursing home and Grandma. A few miles of silence passed, then Mom said, "I guess we weren't running so late after all."

"I guess we weren't," I agreed quietly, remembering the voice. *Thank You, Lord, for using us as instruments of Your mercy.*

PROMISE
Sallie Chesham

For him who looks
And listens,
Eternity glistens
With songshine.

Four

THE

AMAZING

COINCIDENCES

*T*he steps of a man are from the Lord.

        —Psalm 37:23, RSV

As Christians we believe that our times are in God's hands (Psalm 31:15). Yet we are often surprised at the unexpected meetings, the exact timings, and the beautiful matchings that occur in our lives. God's coincidences deal with such mundane things as brake shoes and such important things as a baby's name. They reach around the world and through the years, from Ecuador to Timbuktu, from India to Maine, from Mississippi to Alaska, proving that for the Christian there are really no coincidences, just God-incidents.

To the Ends of the Earth
Stephen Saint

For years I'd thought Timbuktu was just a made-up name for "the ends of the earth." When I found out it was a real place in Africa, I developed an inexplicable fascination for it. It was in 1986 on a fact-finding trip to West Africa for Mission Aviation Fellowship that this fascination became an irresistible urge. Timbuktu wasn't on my itinerary, but I knew I *had* to go there. Once I arrived, however, I discovered I was in trouble.

I'd hitched a ride from Bamako, Mali, five hundred miles away, on the only seat left on a Navajo six-seater airplane chartered by UNICEF. Two of their doctors were in Timbuktu and might fly back on the return flight, which meant I'd be bumped, but I decided to take the chance.

Now here I was, standing by the plane on the windswept outskirts of the famous Berber outpost. There was not a spot of true green anywhere in the desolate brown Saharan landscape. Dust blew across the sky, blotting out the sun as I squinted in the 110-degree heat, trying to make out the mud-walled buildings of the village of twenty thousand.

The pilot approached me as I started for town. He reported that the doctors were on their way and I'd have to find another ride to Bamako. "Try the marketplace. Someone there might have a truck. But be careful," he said. "Westerners don't last long in the desert if the truck breaks down, which often happens."

I didn't relish the thought of being stranded, but perhaps it was fitting that I should wind up like this, surrounded by the Sahara. Since I arrived in Africa the strain of the harsh environment and severe suffering of the starving peoples had left me feeling lost in a spiritual and emotional desert.

The open-air marketplace in the center of town was crowded. Men and women wore flowing robes and turbans as protection against the sun. Most of the Berbers' robes were dark blue, with thirty feet of material in their turbans alone. The men were well-armed with scimitars and knives. I felt that eyes were watching me suspiciously.

Suspicion was understandable in Timbuktu. Nothing could be trusted here. These people had once been prosperous and self-sufficient. Now even their land had turned against them. Drought had turned rich grasslands to desert. Unrelenting sun and windstorms had nearly annihilated all animal life. People were dying by the thousands.

I went from person to person trying to find someone who spoke English, until I finally came across a local gendarme who understood my broken French.

"I need a truck," I said. "I need to go to Bamako."

Eyes widened in his shaded face. "No truck," he shrugged. Then he added, "No road. Only sand."

By now, my presence was causing a sensation in the marketplace. I was surrounded by at least a dozen small children, jumping and dancing, begging for coins and souvenirs. The situation was extreme, I knew. I tried to think calmly. *What am I to do?*

Suddenly I had a powerful desire to talk to my father. Certainly he had known what it was like to be a foreigner in a strange land. But my father, Nate Saint, was dead. He was one of five missionary men killed by Auca Indians in the jungles of Ecuador in 1956. I was a month shy of my fifth birthday at the time, and my memories of him were almost like movie clips: a lanky, intense man with a serious goal and a quick wit. He was a dedicated jungle pilot, flying missionaries and medical personnel in his Piper Family Cruiser. Even after his death he was a presence in my life.

I'd felt the need to talk with my father before, especially since I'd married and become a father myself. But in recent weeks this need had become urgent. For one thing, I was new to relief work. But it was more than that. I needed Dad to help answer my new questions of faith.

In Mali, for the first time in my life, I was surrounded by people who didn't share my faith, who were, in fact, hostile to the Christian faith—locals and Western relief workers alike. In a way it was a parallel to the situation Dad had faced in Ecuador. How often I'd said the same thing Dad would have said among the Indians who killed him: "My God is real. He's a personal God who lives inside me, with whom I have a very special, one-on-one relationship."

And yet the question lingered in my mind: *Did my father have to die?*

All my life, people had spoken of Dad with respect; he was a man willing to die for his faith. But at the time I couldn't help but think the murders were capricious, an accident of bad timing. Dad and his colleagues landed just as a small band of Auca men were in a bad mood for reasons that had nothing to do with faith or Americans. If Dad's plane had landed one day later, the massacre might not have happened.

Couldn't there have been another way? It made little impact on the Aucas that I could see. To them it was just one more killing in a history of killings.

Thirty years later it still had an impact on to me. And now, for the first time, I felt threatened because of who I was and what I believed. "God," I found myself praying as I looked around the marketplace, "I'm in trouble here. Please keep me safe and show me a way to get back. Please reveal Yourself and Your love to me the way you did to my father."

No bolt of lightning came from the blue. But a new thought did come to mind. Surely there was a telecommunications office here somewhere; I could wire Bamako to send another plane. It would be costly, but I could see no other way of getting out. "Where's the telecommunications office?" I asked another gendarme. He gave me instructions, then said, "Telegraph transmits only. If station in Bamako has machine on, message goes through. If not . . ." he shrugged. "No answer ever comes. You only hope message received."

Now what? The sun was crossing toward the horizon. If I didn't have arrangements made by nightfall, what would happen to me? This was truly the last outpost of the world. More than a few Westerners had disappeared in the desert without a trace.

Then I remembered that just before I'd started for Timbuktu, a fellow worker had said, "There's a famous mosque in Timbuktu. It was built from mud in the 1500s. Many Islamic pilgrims visit it every year. But there's also a tiny Christian church, which virtually no one visits. Look it up if you get the chance."

I asked the children, "Where is *l'église Évangelique Chrétienne?*" The youngsters were willing to help, though they were obviously confused about what I was looking for. Several times elderly men and women scolded them harshly as we passed, but they persisted. Finally we arrived, not at the church, but at the open doorway of a tiny mud-brick house. No one was home, but on the wall opposite the door was a poster showing a cross covered by wounded hands. The French subscript said, "and by His stripes we are healed."

Within minutes, my army of waifs pointed out a young man approaching us in the dirt alleyway. Then the children melted back into the labyrinth of the walled alleys and compounds of Timbuktu.

The young man was handsome, with dark skin and flowing robes. But there was something inexplicably different about him. His name was Nouh Ag Infa Yatara; that much I understood. Nouh signaled he knew someone who could translate for us. He led me to a compound on the edge of town where an American missionary lived. I was glad to meet the missionary, but from the moment I'd seen Nouh I'd had the feeling that we shared something in common.

"How did you come to have faith?" I asked him.

The missionary translated as Nouh answered. "This compound has always had a beautiful garden. One day when I was a small boy, a friend and I decided to steal some carrots. It was a dangerous task. We'd been told that *Toubabs* [white men] eat nomadic children. Despite our agility and considerable experience, I was caught by the former missionary here. Mr. Marshall didn't eat me; instead he gave me the carrots and some cards that had God's promises from the Bible written on them. He said if I learned them, he'd give me an ink pen!"

"You learned them?" I asked.

"Oh, yes! Only government men and the headmaster of the school had a Bic pen! But when I showed off my pen at school, the teacher knew I must have spoken with a Toubab, which is strictly forbidden. He severely beat me."

When Nouh's parents found out he had portions of such a despised book defiling their house, they threw him out and forbade anyone to take him in; nor was he allowed in school. But something had happened: Nouh had come to believe what the Bible said was true.

Nouh's mother became desperate. Her own standing, as well as her family's, was in jeopardy. Finally she decided to kill her son. She obtained poison from a sorcerer and poisoned Nouh's food at a family feast. Nouh ate the food and wasn't affected. His brother, who unwittingly stole a morsel of meat from the deadly dish, became violently ill and remains partially paralyzed. Seeing God's intervention, the family and the townspeople were afraid to make further attempts on his life, but condemned him as an outcast.

After sitting a moment, I asked Nouh the question that only hours earlier I'd wanted to ask my father: "Why is your faith so important to you that you're willing to give up everything, perhaps even your life?"

"I know God loves me and I'll live with Him forever. I *know* it! Now I have peace where I used to be full of fear and uncertainty. Who wouldn't give up everything for this peace and security?"

"It can't have been easy for you as a teenager to take a stand that made you despised by the whole community," I said. "Where did your courage come from?"

"Mr. Marshall couldn't take me in without putting my life in jeopardy. So he gave me some books about other Christians who'd suffered for their faith. My favorite was about five young men who willingly risked their lives to take God's good news to stone age Indians in the jungles of South America." His eyes widened. "I've lived all my life in the desert. How frightening the jungle must be! The book said these men let themselves be speared to death, even though they had guns and could have killed their attackers!"

The missionary said, "I remember the story. As a matter of fact, one of those men had your last name."

"Yes," I said quietly, "the pilot was my father."

"Your father?" Nouh cried. "The story is true!"

"Yes," I said, "it's true."

The missionary and Nouh and I talked through the afternoon. When they accompanied me back to the airfield that night, we found that the doctors weren't able to leave Timbuktu after all, and there was room for me on the UNICEF plane.

As Nouh and I hugged each other, it seemed incredible that God loved us so much that He'd arranged for us to meet "at the ends of the earth." Nouh and I had gifts for each other that no one else could give. I gave him the assurance that the story that had given him courage was true. He gave me the assurance that God *had* used Dad's death for good. Dad, by dying, had helped give Nouh a faith worth dying for. And Nouh, in return, had helped give Dad's faith back to me.

AFTER FIFTY YEARS
Edward A. Elliott

*I*t meant a day out of our vacation, but my wife and I strongly felt that we should make the effort while we were in Maine to go see Dr. Reuben Larson, an eighty-year-old missionary pioneer. After lunch during our visit, quite out of the blue, Dr. Larson asked, "Ed, in all your travels have you ever run into an Indian named Bakht Singh?"

How extraordinary! Only two weeks before, on one of his infrequent visits to the United States, Bakht Singh had invited me to lunch. I told Dr. Larson what I'd learned about Singh, how he was one of India's best-known Christian leaders, how he had founded hundreds of churches and had preached to thousands. Whenever he traveled, believers gathered at train stations to speak and pray with him for just a few minutes.

The things I told about this godly man had a strange effect on Dr. Larson. He was literally openmouthed. Finally he explained why.

"Many years ago in western Canada I met a young Indian engineering student who was interested in the Christian faith. His name was Bakht Singh. For fifty years I've been praying for him, praying that he would come to know God better and serve Him. I've always wondered what became of him."

It wasn't long after our visit that Dr. Larson died. But even before then I knew why we'd taken that day out of our vacation to see him. We were meant to bring him the news that he had waited fifty years to hear.

CAR TROUBLE
Ron Bailey

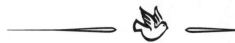

The other day the wife and I were talking with a neighbor, and the subject of feeling close to God came up. Immediately I thought of one time in particular, a time of great uncertainty for Carolyn and me. It was the spring of 1955, early in our marriage. Carolyn was eighteen, I was twenty-two, and our first child, Karen, was a year old. I had just finished my tour of duty with the Navy in San Diego, and we were heading home to Tacoma, Washington.

Packing and getting on the road had worn us out. We had only enough money for gas and groceries. My separation check from the Navy would be mailed to my folks' home in Tacoma. And then what? we wondered. I had no trade, no job. How would we get by? This was in our minds and in our conversation on the road back home. Frankly, there weren't any answers, and that was scary.

"I'm exhausted," I said to Carolyn.

"Me too," she replied wearily as she tried to soothe our fretting baby girl.

Dusk had fallen in the Siskiyou Mountains. Pulling our eight-year-old business coupe into a clearing by the roadside, we camped for the night in the twenty-one-foot trailer hitched behind the car. The trailer had been our home in California, and we were pulling it to Tacoma with us.

We were miles from any town, along a two-lane road that led through the mountains of northern California. Not much traffic passed along this stretch except for an occasional truck whizzing—a little too fast, I thought—around the curves.

Early the next morning, just after breakfast, I noticed it: a big black 1937 Buick sedan stopped right at the bend of the road. "What a strange place for anyone to stop," I said to Carolyn. "You'd think the driver would know better."

The car was half on, half off the road. No one could pass without going into the opposite lane. And one of those big trucks might be coming around the bend . . .

"Carolyn, I'm going to go up and speak to those people about moving their car." I had seen a man get out and go to the back of the car, then a woman. As I approached, they both looked frustrated. Hopeless, you might say. A boy of about six was looking out of the window.

"This is a dangerous stopping point," I called out.

"I can't get it to move," the man said to me. "It just locked up. I think it's this back wheel. But I tell you, it won't move."

"Well, maybe you should try pushing it off the road."

"It won't move," he said again helplessly.

"Got any tools?" I asked the man.

"Well, no, ah . . . I'm not very mechanical, I'm afraid. We're on our way to Oregon, where I have a job prospect. This couldn't have happened at a worse time."

All of their possessions were inside the car and strapped on top of it. It was clear that this young family had been struggling. Everything about them spoke of their need. The old car. Well-worn clothes. Belongings that most people would yard-sale today. That job prospect was their only hope, and now, with barely enough money for gas, they were faced with car trouble.

I directed the man to go up the road and the woman to go down the road to warn approaching traffic. Then I got my tools, jacked up the Buick and took off the rear wheel.

The brake linings had wedged over one another and had forced the round drum into an ellipse that was locked in place. I forced off the brake drum with a pry bar and hammer.

Brake drum, brake shoes, lining—all useless. Then I bolted the wheel back on, and we coasted the car down to our trailer so that I could work on it.

It would take some sort of invention to put this family, desperate to get to that job interview, back on the road. "The best I can do," I said to the man and his wife, "is to pinch off the brake tube to this wheel so you won't lose fluid when you press the brake pedal. That means you'll have three wheels with brakes and one without. That will get you to the nearest town, but you must stop there and replace the drum and brake shoes."

I could see the worried looks cross their faces. I figured the reason—they didn't have the money for parts or repairs. "Do you have any relatives or friends in this part of the country?" I asked.

"No," said the man. "No one."

Carolyn and I didn't have much either, but at least we were heading toward family.

"Well, on this mountain road you can't drive very far with only three working brakes. It's just too dangerous . . ." I still hadn't figured how I would close off the brake tube to that one wheel. Maybe I could make something to cap it. Or pinch it shut. As I was considering possibilities, the couple's little boy ran up. He'd been playing just down the bank.

"Daddy, Daddy—" In his excitement he could hardly get his breath. "There's a car down the bank, and it's just like ours!"

"Oh, Son," said his father, a bit wearily, "it may look like ours, but it isn't." His mind was far away, somewhere up the road, at the next town, wondering how he was going to buy the parts he needed to get them to Oregon.

"Son, you just think it looks like ours. Now you run and play. We've got to fix this car somehow."

"But Daddy, it *is* just like ours!"

He was so positive that I said to the man, "Why don't we just have a look? It couldn't hurt."

The car was overturned about sixty feet down the embankment, and as we climbed down I could see that it had landed near some large boulders near a river. The engine and transmission were missing—taken by scavengers. So were the wheels.

But as I inspected it, the man and I looked at each other. Our curiosity turned to wonder. The car was *identical* to his. Same model, same year, same color. And though the wheels were missing, the brake drums were still intact.

I had brought my pry bar and hammer and some wrenches, and I busied myself in taking off the brake drum that was closest. I was balancing on the rocks and working with the wrenches while the man and his son poked around the car.

"Could I borrow that pry bar?" the man asked.

"Sure," I said and handed it over.

Intent on my work and still thinking about the coincidence of an identical wreck being at the exact spot in the road where this man's car broke down, I heard the two working with the pry bar to open the trunk of this old hulk. Still locked, or rusted shut after all these years . . .

Then I heard the creaking sounds of the trunk hinges opening. "Hey, there's a lug wrench!" shouted the man. "I could sure use that . . . and there's a paper bag." I heard the rustling of paper. And then silence.

The man came around to where I was working. He stared at me for a moment. I could tell it was difficult for him to speak. He held a brown paper sack.

"Do you have any idea what's in this sack?" he asked finally.

He stood there swallowing hard, trying not to cry. "Here . . . see? New brake shoes!"

With the necessary parts provided, I repaired their car, Carolyn fixed them a meal, and they started off down the road, waving. Alone? Helpless? Not at all. You see, I knew that Somebody upstairs cared very much for those three, and He was providing for their every need.

Right then and there, things no longer seemed so uncertain for Carolyn and me and Karen, either. For I also knew that if God could provide for those people, He could provide for us.

And as I was telling my neighbor the other day, for thirty-five years He has done just that.

In Full Supply
Jacqueline Hewitt Allen

Y ears and years ago, my grandmother told me a story out of her past that I always think of at gift-giving time, especially at Christmas. I remember sitting in her lap as dark-eyed little Sue Belle Johnson, my grandmother, explained how, shortly after the turn of the century, at remote and often lonely stations across the United States and overseas, missionaries and their families lived lives of hardship, privation, and isolation in their efforts to carry the gospel to people most of us would never know or see.

Probably at no time of the year were their feelings of isolation and loneliness more keenly felt than at Christmas. To remember them at this season, the custom in those days was for churches to send what were called "missionary barrels" to missionaries in remote locations.

The missionary and his wife would sit down with their children and make a list of things they wanted for Christmas.

The list would include articles of clothing, toys, perhaps books or household utensils—whatever they especially needed but could not afford or could not find to buy. The list also included the ages of the children and their clothing sizes.

When completed, the list was sent to the missionary organization that helped sponsor them. The organization in turn sent it to a church, whose members would then take it upon themselves to acquire the items on the list.

My grandmother's church in Hattiesburg, Mississippi, was one of the churches that received such a Christmas list. That particular year, the list came from a missionary family in what was then called Indian Territory. The women of Grandmother's church, many of them, saw it as a holy task to choose an item and either buy it, make it, or donate money for its purchase.

On an appointed day all the requested items would be brought to the church, and the women would check the items against the list, wrap them, and pack them into a big wooden-staved, double-ended barrel. The barrel would then be shipped in time for the family to receive it by Christmas.

Not everybody in Grandmother's church cooperated. While the women were packing the missionary barrel, one of the more well-to-do women of the church walked into the room carrying a coat. "I've got this coat of my husband's that I want to give to you," she announced offhandedly. "I'm going to buy him a new one."

Grandmother was appalled. She didn't say anything, but she was thinking plenty: *These other people have worked hard to get these articles, some have sacrificed to get them, and here this woman is in effect bragging, "I'm so rich I can go out and buy another coat."*

The more she thought about the woman's haughtiness, the more irritated Grandmother became. *She's just ridding herself of an unwanted castoff,* Grandmother said to herself. *What kind of Christmas attitude is that?* Grandmother was furious—about the coat and with the woman.

A coat was not on the missionary family's list, and the women packing the barrel had no intention of putting the coat in it. But after all the requested items had been carefully placed in the barrel, there was still room left.

"Well," one of the women said, "let's put that coat in. It might help keep the other articles tight, keep them from bouncing around and maybe breaking."

So, they folded the coat, packed it in, and closed the barrel. Then they shipped it to the family out in the Indian Territory.

Weeks passed. Christmas came and went. Then a letter arrived at the church: the family's thank-you, written by the missionary's wife. "Dear Friends," it began, "we want to thank you for the barrel."

She then recounted how her husband and their three children had driven to the railhead to pick up the barrel, had brought it home and placed it upright in the middle of the living room floor in their little cabin, waiting for Christmas. The children were so excited they danced around it in gleeful anticipation.

Then on the day before Christmas a fierce winter storm blew in. It quickly developed into a blizzard, with snow so thick and winds so furious that the entire outdoors seemed a blowing, blinding mass of white. Shortly before suppertime, as the blizzard raged, there was a banging on the front door, and when the missionary opened the door to see what the banging was, there stood an old man, grizzled, ill clad for the freezing temperature, shivering and covered with snow.

"I'm lost," the man said. "Could I come in for a while?"

The missionary opened the door wider and said, "Of course. Come on in."

After supper, it was all but impossible to contain the children, they were so excited and eager to open the barrel. But their mother managed to get them bedded down, explaining that they would have to wait a little longer, since it would be terribly impolite to open the barrel, pull out the presents, and distribute them with the old man there. "There's nothing for him," the mother said. "It's just the things we put on our list. We'll have to wait till the man leaves."

The next morning, Christmas morning, the family arose and found that the storm had not abated; the winds were as wild as the night before. The mother fixed a special breakfast for everyone, and when breakfast was over, they watched and waited for the storm to end so that the old man could be on his way and they could break open the barrel.

Afternoon came and the storm was still raging, but the children just couldn't wait any longer. So the missionary and his wife explained to the old man that the barrel had been packed many weeks earlier and contained Christmas presents for the family only. They apologized profusely, and when the old man nodded and said he understood, the missionary turned to the barrel and began to break open the uppermost end of it.

The family then began pulling out, one by one, the items they had asked for on their Christmas list. Each item was clearly marked so that they all knew whose present it was. Everyone was excited. The clothes, the toys, everything, were exactly what the family had requested. Everyone was happy and pleased, while the old man sat and watched.

Finally they reached the bottom of the barrel. There on the bottom, at the end of the barrel that had been uppermost when the women packed it, was an item the family didn't recognize. It was nothing they had asked for. When the missionary reached deep into the barrel to pull out the object, he could see it was a man's coat. He held it up. It looked to be about the size of the old man. "Try it on." The man took it and slipped it on. It fit perfectly. "It must be for you," the missionary told him, smiling.

"How did you ever know," the missionary wife's letter concluded, "that we would need a man's coat for Christmas? Thank you all so very much."

By the time she finished reading the letter, my grandmother said, she was nearly overcome with awe. The cast-off coat that had needed a new owner had found one. An old man who had needed a warm coat had been given one. A family who had taken in a lost stranger and needed a special present for him had been provided with one. It was all too marvelous to comprehend, my grandmother said. Surely God, in His wondrous omniscience, she said, had wrought a miracle with a gift she had thought unworthy.

When she finished her story, grandmother took my hands in hers and said, "I learned that day that I had been wrong—and that I should never despise a gift that God can use."

As Christmas approaches again, I'm remembering once more my grandmother's words. As I choose presents to give this Christmas, I am hoping that they will be gifts that will make the recipients happy and me proud to give. But most of all I am praying that, whatever they are, whomever they're for, they will be exactly the gifts that God can use.

THE AFTERTHOUGHT
Carol Knapp

For weeks my husband, Terry, had been preparing to run the Iron Dog, a snowmobile race held each February following Alaska's famed Iditarod sled dog trail. It's one thousand miles of snow and ice, bitter cold, and treacherous mountain passes. Terry's gear was ready, his partner, GW, was waiting at the start on nearby Big Lake. Scanning the shop one last time, his eyes fell on a hacksaw. Thinking it might be handy to have, he packed it.

By the end of the first day the two of them had reached the Kuskokwim River, one hundred and twenty-five miles into the wilderness. Anxious to take the lead, GW hit a patch of open water in the dark. The rear end of his snowmobile fell back into the frigid river. He stepped off, sinking to his armpits in the black water before scrambling up onto the solid ice. His gear was submerged, he was soaked to the skin, and the temperature had dipped to twenty degrees below zero.

Terry's first thought was to build a fire and try to warm GW before hypothermia set in. Unfortunately, the ax was also in the river. Then Terry remembered the hacksaw he'd hastily stuffed in his pack. It wasn't much, but with it he cut down some small trees and eventually had a fire blazing. Terry spent a memorable night holed up on the frozen river, trying to dry out his impetuous partner.

That hacksaw, an afterthought, helped save a life. But was it really a last-minute choice, or did God plan for it to be included all along? Was His grace at work behind the scenes?

Stamp of Approval
B. J. Connor

*W*e called the newborn Brandon. He wasn't supposed to stay with us for very long. Our three previous foster children had been adopted after a short time, but by November Brandon had been with us for seven months and I was getting anxious. The longer he stayed, the more my husband and I and our two children loved him. He was a gorgeous baby, healthy and good-natured and going through those delightful early stages of life that his permanent family should have had the privilege of enjoying.

"What's taking so long?" I asked God impatiently. I knew the adoption agency we were associated with, Bethany Christian Services, was working hard to find just the right parents for him, but he needed to be adopted soon, while he would go willingly to others without crying about leaving us.

Though we hadn't fostered with the intention of adopting a child ourselves, my husband, Michael, and I began to wonder if, since we loved Brandon so much, perhaps the agency might make an exception and let us, a white family, adopt this beautiful black child. I didn't think adopting was what God wanted us to do, so I decided to move things along. I called friends who might be, or know of, prospective parents for Brandon. Part of me said the Lord was in control of this dear child's life, but another part of me muttered that He was sure taking His own sweet time about it.

Then one night the phone rang. "BJ," our social worker said, "I think we have a couple for Brandon in another state, and they sound wonderful!"

Her announcement caught me off guard. "How soon do you think it will be?" I asked, surprised at how disappointed I felt.

"In a few weeks," she said. "You know how unpredictable it is with all this paperwork, especially with an interstate placement."

From that moment on, each day with Brandon took on a bittersweet poignancy. We watched even more carefully as Brandon entertained us with his gummy smiles and Da-Da's, his jabbering and sputtering. I continued to write in his baby book and date his baby pictures.

I lingered on the Halloween photos of Brandon with a big

Mexican sombrero on his head and an improvised striped dishtowel serape on his shoulders. Too bad we couldn't let his family know we'd dubbed him "Brandon Burrito." The adoptive parents were to receive him as a "blank slate" and name him themselves.

On his last morning with us, a cold, wet one, we bundled Brandon up and rode with the social worker to the airport in the gloomy darkness. At the gate we eagerly scanned the disembarking passengers until we spotted an attractive young black couple carrying a diaper bag and no baby. "I think this little guy's for you," I said as they approached.

The slender woman reached for Brandon, and he went easily to her. He began grasping at her glasses. "He loves glasses," we chorused.

After quick introductions, we drove to the agency's office, which had homey rooms where the couple could get acquainted with their new son. The couple told us of their frustrating two-and-a-half-year quest to adopt—until they linked up with the branch of Bethany Christian Services in their state.

Then they received a letter from our branch, she said, and "something told me a picture of the baby was in that envelope. I went into the house and told my husband, 'Our baby's in here.' " They opened the envelope and out fell a picture of our Brandon.

We left the three of them to have time alone while we went to lunch. When we left, Brandon's new mom was spooning a jar of sweet potatoes into him.

While we were gone, I found myself worrying about Brandon, especially because he had missed his nap. But when we returned, I heard the cheery sound of Brandon's familiar chortling. He was on his back on his quilt, playing with his feet, amusing his parents as he had so often amused us.

Finally there was a flurry of document signing, and we were off to the airport again. On the sidewalk, we gave good-bye hugs to our beloved Brandon and to our new friends, knowing we'd probably never see any of them again.

The last memory I have of them is the backs of a man and a woman, a little hooded face peering out over her shoulder, going through the door of the terminal. God had brought them together in His own time, with a plan even more wonderful than I ever could have imagined. I knew that for certain when one of us asked, "What are you going to name him?"

"Brandon," his mother replied. "What did you call him?"

THE SUDDEN FREEZE
Agnes Huyser

When my husband, Quincy, and I bought a farm and moved to Gallatin Gateway in April 1964, I couldn't wait to get unpacked. I had to plant my vegetable garden by May.

I needed some extra confidence this time, since I had never planted a garden so close to the mountains before and I wasn't "onto" the sudden nighttime temperature changes that wreak havoc on plants.

I enjoyed planting a big garden, but I also felt it was a necessity. With thirteen growing children to feed, I had to make my contribution to our family's health and finances. My garden would provide us with enough vegetables for canning to see us through the next winter.

Quincy and the boys worked hard on our five hundred acres, tending the beef and milk cows, chickens and pigs. The girls and I cultivated the garden, planted seeds, weeded, and watered. There was hardly a vegetable in a seed catalog for our altitude that I didn't have in my garden.

Our new home abutted the foot hills of snowcapped peaks seventy miles from Yellowstone National Park. I looked forward to a family outing there to see the roaring waterfalls, the hot spouting geysers, the cold sparkling rivers and the antelope, elk and other wildlife.

We were now also only ten miles from my mom and dad. Their deep faith had rubbed off on me, and when I poked a tiny carrot seed in the soft earth, I felt the Lord was kneeling right beside me, getting His knees and hands dirty too. I thought I had a no-fail crop-insurance policy.

True, I put in long hours, and when canning season arrived, I'd often be working till midnight canning tomatoes, beans, or whatever was ripe at the time. But I really enjoyed it, and I knew that when winter came, I'd be able to go down cellar to get three or four quarts of vegetables for supper. I'd linger and feast my eyes on the thousand-plus quarts of ruby red beets, green beans, golden corn, peas, carrots, and strawberries, to name a few, that I had provided for my family.

By August I knew my garden would be a winner again; one hundred fifty quarts of green beans were already canned and on the shelves. We always did the beans "assembly line"—I'd pick the tender vines, and the girls would cut and snap, joking and talking nonstop under the old willow tree in the yard. The deep satisfaction I felt packing the jars and processing made the hot, steamy job worth every bead of sweat.

Making pickles was next, and *that* job was a real labor of love. Our kids insisted I pack a pickle in their school lunches, and if I forgot, I'd hear about it. Deep down, I was flattered. That summer, though, the dill came up poorly, yellowish and unfit for pickling. I blamed it on the black gumbo soil. But

Mom and Dad had plenty of "volunteer" dill that had resown itself, so by late August I placed an SOS phone call.

"Mom, I have a terrific crop of cucumbers! Can you spare some dill for pickles?"

They drove up before I had a chance to pick the cucumbers. The kids had already scattered to the pasture, well into their usual after-supper baseball game. Mom carried in a big brown paper bag full to bulging with the most beautiful green dill I had ever seen. She set it down in the entryway, and we visited and watched the kids in the field. At dusk the folks drove off.

"I'll pick the cukes first thing in the morning," I yawned at Quincy. "It's too dark out in the garden now."

But I never did get to pick them. The next morning as I neared the garden, I stopped in my tracks when I saw the devastation before me. A hard freeze had stolen in during the night. Yesterday's firm, perky cucumber leaves were like limp, wet rags, hiding soft, mushy cucumbers below. The patch was a total loss.

I hurried to the staked-up tomatoes. Yesterday they were green and some were turning, ready to be brought inside to ripen. Today they too were mushy, black and glassy.

I was heartsick. This was a tremendous loss to our food supply. And all that time and effort wasted! I felt I had let the family and myself down. If only I'd stayed up and listened to the weather report on the late news. Truth is, even if I had remembered, I had been too tired.

I berated myself all day for not having gone out and picked the cucumbers by flashlight. And that night, I tossed and turned, feeling quite alone, though Quincy was sleeping peacefully beside me. Despite my carefully nurtured faith in the Lord, I wasn't accepting this disapointment gracefully. The Lord knew how hard I had worked to do the right thing by my family.

Like a broken record, I was tormenting myself with if-onlys when I heard a gentle voice saying, "Agnes, who feeds you and your family?" Was I hearing things? Everyone else was asleep. Then I decided it could be only one Person speaking to me.

I paused before whispering weakly, "Well, God, You do." Then I added as if to affirm my faith, "I know it all comes from You."

It was a while before the voice continued, "Does it really matter if it comes out of *your* garden or not?"

That question took me by surprise and I giggled. "God, I guess it doesn't really matter whether or not it comes from my garden. I know it all comes from You." With that I was given total peace, and I fell asleep.

The next day I was still puzzled by the Lord's question. For days I hoped someone in the valley would have a bumper crop of cucumbers and I'd be able to fill the pickle jars. But no cucumbers, much less tomatoes, came my way.

Eventually I got tired of looking at the bag of dill mocking me in the entryway. One day I jammed another bag over the top and placed the dill out of sight on a roughed-in ledge by the stairs leading to the cellar.

The following winter brought a bitter cold snap that hung over the valley. By the end of February, the temperature hovered at twenty below, snow lay frozen on the ground, and driving was treacherous on the mountain curves. The days were short, so it was dark when we sat down for our evening meals.

Late one afternoon I went down cellar to get vegetables for supper and noted with dismay how bare the shelves looked. The corn, beans, and peas were going fast. And where there should have been tomatoes and pickles was row after row of empty, dusty jars. Going back upstairs, I shook my head as I passed the bag of dill. Then I busied myself at the stove.

Suppertime was my family's favorite time of the day. All fifteen of us sat around a huge oblong table that had been Quincy's mother's. I always spread the table with the prettiest oilcloth I could find. Quincy had made two long padded benches, covered in a cheerful orange, the color of glowing embers. Our oversize kitchen was warm and cozy from the old Monarch wood-and-coal stove that I cooked on.

We were having a delightful meal, the kids recounting what happened at school, when someone pounded hard on the door. I pushed my chair back, mumbling, "Who in the world would be out in this bitter cold—and in the dark too?"

Standing in the entryway was one of our neighbors, a man in his late thirties with a full dark beard that was glazed and white with frost. He looked like Santa Claus.

"Mrs. Huyser," he said as he stepped into the warm kitchen, "how many fresh cucumbers and tomatoes can you use?"

The clatter of knives and forks ceased. All eyes fastened on our bearded visitor. With my mouth agape, I thought, *Did I hear right?* Fresh cucumbers and tomatoes in February? I was speechless.

"I have a two-ton truck outside more than half full with cucumbers, tomatoes, green beans—even eggplant." Quincy and I zipped up our winter jackets, tugged on mittens, and trudged out to look.

Our neighbor's teeth were on the verge of chattering, but his soft voice was steady and clear. "The produce was on its way from Mexico, but the road coming down the canyon was so icy that the truck slid into the Gallatin River."

"How come it didn't freeze?" I blurted.

"All the boxes that landed on the bank did freeze, but the ones that went in the river were okay. The insurance company hired me to get the truck out and let me keep whatever I wanted. So I salvaged this stuff." He thumped the side of the truck. "I figured you could use some of this with your big family. The only thing is," he added somewhat apologetically, "my wife will want the green beans since she didn't get to can any last summer."

I managed to say, "That's one thing I *did* can."

We packed in nine big boxes of beautiful Beefsteak-size

tomatoes and box after box of firm, green, perfect-for-pickling cucumbers, and the next day I prepared for canning.

I was surprised that some of the dill was still green, and the rest revived in a warm water bath. By early March I had canned ninety-two quarts of ice pickles, bread-and-butter pickles, and, of course, crisp dills. It was the only time I had ever been able to "play" at pickling, not pressured to can everything at once, as I was at harvesttime.

I was putting up the pickles when I remembered what the Lord had said to me seven months before: "Does it really matter if it comes out of *your* garden or not?" And when I answered, "I know it all comes from You," I didn't dream it would come from an ice-cold, fast-flowing mountain river.

But then I don't even *try* to fathom His ways. I simply don't have the imagination.

WHEN DAD CHANGED HIS MIND
Muriel Lombardi

My father was born at 740 East 216th Street in the Bronx in New York City. This was the home where he brought my mother after their marriage. Here he and Mom raised their five children; here he grew his vegetable garden and brought the stray dogs and cats he was always picking up. Here was the neighborhood he knew so well, first as a postman, then in his retirement, walking five miles every day, greeting neighbors, buying groceries, attending Mass every morning.

As Mom and Dad grew older, we worried that the old house was too much for them to keep up, but whenever we suggested they move into something smaller or closer to us, Dad wouldn't budge. He refused to let go of his beloved 740.

When Dad turned seventy-nine, his health declined and he had to be taken to the hospital. Yet after a week he returned home to tend his garden and help Mom keep house. One day, however, when Dad was back in the hospital my sister-in-law received a call from him that took her by surprise. "It's time to sell the house," he told her. That was the last conversation he had with her, for several hours later Dad died of a sudden heart attack.

Grief-stricken, I drove to the hospital to collect Dad's things. Just as I was about to go into his room, I stopped, and as I stared at the number on his door, I had an odd feeling that was somehow comforting. Dad's room number was 740.

CHANGES

June Hauvermale

Things change.

Friendships fade,
Money is spent,
Glory's forgotten,
Power is lost.

Seasons change,
So do people,
Day turns to darkness,
Sorrow to joy.

Pain is eased,
Rules are broken,
Promises forgotten,
Trust betrayed.

Life ends,
Love cools,
Hate dies,
Stars fall.

Things change . . .
But God is always God.

Five

THE

GLORIOUS

IMPOSSIBLE

Good] is able to do exceeding abundantly above all that we ask or think.

—*Ephesians 3:20*

"God specializes in things thought impossible," says the old Gospel song by Oscar Eliason. The stories in this section demonstrate the truth of that quotation. Cars that pull off to rest on nonexistent highway shoulders, words spoken through a nonexistent voicebox, an almost frozen transmission that runs like a dream for years—these are some of the wonderful happenings that caused the participants to give glory to God.

HIS BROAD SHOULDERS
Helene Lewis Coffer

*L*ean on the Lord," friends in our prayer group urged us. "His shoulders are broad."

At the time, my husband and I needed a shoulder to lean on. Our business had turned sour, our savings were dwindling, and at retirement age, we were scrounging for jobs. In the midst of this, my ninety-four-year-old mother experienced a mental and physical breakdown. Living with my sister in southwestern Arizona, she required twenty-four-hour care, and now it looked as if she needed to be put into a nursing home.

One Sunday night I was praying about our problems as I drove home alone from my sister's after a week spent helping with Mom's care. The narrow two-lane road was heavy with traffic coming from Las Vegas, the headlights blinding my eyes. Three different times I came over hills to find a driver coming at me in my lane, and I had to pull off the side of the road to avoid a collision. I don't mind telling you I was thankful that *those* broad shoulders were there.

Two weeks later I made the same trip with my husband. In full daylight we reached the road just north of Kingman, Arizona. "This was the stretch," I told him, "where I had to pull off."

We looked and looked, and grew quieter and quieter.

For that entire forty-mile section of Highway 93, cactus and greasewood and mesquite grow close to the roadside. There were no shoulders—only His to lean on.

Out of Control!
Andrew C. Sorelle, Jr.

After the invasion of France in 1944 our outfit, the 48th Fighter Group, 9th Air Force, was one of the first to be moved to Normandy. A steel matted flying strip was laid out for us through apple orchards and hedgerows. We were flying several missions each day in support of our front line troops.

About noon one day in early July, Operations received orders to send four Thunderbolts to attack a column of German trucks. It was a typical mission except for one thing: the weather was very bad. The enemy was taking advantage of the weather to retreat, hoping that we would not dare to fly in the prevailing weather conditions.

The four of us took off and stayed low, just beneath the cloud ceiling. Just as we came over the top of a hill, there they were—trucks and equipment, bumper to bumper on the highway below. We did not have the advantage of surprise, because after we spotted the convoy we had to circle and return and by that time the enemy was ready for us. Most of the men had scattered into ditches by the roadside. Others had mounted guns and were firing a crossfire through which we were forced to fly. As we made our run it seemed that the whole overcast day was lit up with German tracers.

All of a sudden I felt a heavy jolt to my plane and immediately it went out of control. A German 88-mm. shell had ripped a three-foot hole through the left wing.

By a miracle the shell, fused to go off on contact, did not

explode. But it did cut the aileron cable. The aileron itself, that all-important tab on the trailing edge of the wing, fell from the plane. I knew in that instant that I had lost my aircraft: 90 percent of my flying control came from the two ailerons; one was gone entirely, and the other was flopping in the wind.

I knew, too, exactly what my plane would do. It would nose down and barrel-roll to the left. Aerodynamically, there was no other possibility and that is precisely what did start to happen. I was only two hundred feet from the ground when the roll started. I knew I was going to die. In the seconds that followed I lived an eternity, waiting for the crash.

What happened next, I am told, could not have happened.

Just a few feet from the ground that battle-torn old Thunderbolt snap-rolled. There were no controls on the aircraft with which such a maneuver could be accomplished, and yet it happened. Instead of barrel-rolling, nose down, to the left, I was making a steep climbing turn to the right, just what I needed to do to return to the airstrip.

My plane continued to do the impossible: it flew into the low overcast and leveled out. I could not see the ground. I didn't care! Somehow I had been given a few extra seconds of time and I wanted to get out of that uncontrollable machine as fast as I could. I threw open the canopy and tried to avoid the wildly gyrating stick as I got loose from all of my harness. I stood up in my seat, just below the slip-stream and tried to go out over the left side of the plane.

But again forces beyond my control took command. Why couldn't I climb out! It was as if I were being physically held back. I looked down into the cockpit—what a mess! My instruments gone, the stick making wild circular movements, and yet my Thunderbolt was flying just as I would have flown it if I had been able. I sat down and buckled up again.

Suddenly I broke out of the overcast and I knew where I was. To my left was the English Channel with barrage balloons, landing craft, warships. And to my right? I looked, knowing what I would see, and there it was: I was approaching my landing strip. I could see the runway just to the right of my plane's nose.

The only control I had left was the tail rudder, which moved the plane right or left. I quickly gave right rudder, which made me do a flat skid that aligned me with the runway. I put the wheels in the down position, and hoped they had dropped. With no instrument panel I could not tell. With no ailerons the only way I could control the attitude of the aircraft was to cut the throttle: that would make me fall. I chopped the throttle hard and the plane fell away beneath me.

I hit perfectly, right at the beginning of the matted runway.

I was going close to one hundred seventy miles per hour. The little Thunderbolt bounced violently and dove toward the runway a second time. Again it bounced and almost nosed over. With each new, violent bounce the end of the matting came closer. The very day before I would have plowed into the hedgerows at the end of the runway, but that night the engineers had come in and bulldozed about two hundred more yards of runway. My plane hit the new mud and started skidding around and around and finally stopped.

After I turned off the ignition switch, I sat quietly in a supernatural hush. In that silence God became real to me. Audibly, or in my spirit, I heard five clear words. "I have saved your life." I knew I was in the indescribable presence of God. Of course, He was there! He had piloted my plane safely home.

The sirens were screaming across the field. I sat, and listened, and as they raced toward me I knew my friends were going to find a different man in the cockpit of that Thunderbolt from the pilot who had climbed aboard an hour earlier. How could it be otherwise? I no longer belonged to myself at all.

"Someone Help Me!"
Mary Virag

I am a farmer's wife. I work often under the open sky, and if I should seek an uninterrupted conversation with the Almighty, I easily could have it for we have no neighbors for miles.

But for a long time I had ceased to pray for God's help because it seemed useless. It was our third straight summer of drought. An early hailstorm had cut down our seedlings in April. Now—with my husband away on a stock-buying trip, with two small children to care for, livestock to feed, and parched crops to be handwatered from the brook—now, on top of everything the house well had run dry. If there was a God in that vast, cloudless sky why couldn't He show some compassion with a little rain?

But there was work to be done. The battle against drought had to go on. I climbed into our three-quarter ton truck, which drags our "watering tank" on a flat wagon behind, and headed for the fields. It was a clumsy, oval, galvanized water tank, but it held a great deal of liquid. There was a three-foot opening on top, through which we filled it by pailfuls from the brook, and through which we could bail out water onto our thirsty crops. The tank was held in place on the flat wagon by several wooden blocks.

On this particular day, our little daughters, Carol and Susie, were with me. They liked to stand on the wagon while they laughingly held onto the swaying, sloshing water tank.

Because of my preoccupied brooding that day, I did not at

first hear their cries. Suddenly their screams were loud in my ears. I looked around but couldn't see anything. I stopped the truck and leaped out.

There, standing on the wagon were Carol and Susie, their faces wild with terror. Then I saw. One of the wooden blocks had slipped and Carol's small bare foot was caught under the tank. Another block midway under the tank was at a weird angle and I could tell that in minutes it, too, would slip and the full weight of the tank would crush her foot.

"Are you hurt?" I cried.

"I don't think so, Mommie. But I can't get loose."

"Don't move!" I commanded.

The wooden block had inched out a little more. I knew there could be no assistance near.

Then I was beside my child, my hand sliding under the small space below the tank till I felt her bare foot against my skin. "Get ready to jump," I panted. I put my shoulder against the heavy tank. It felt cold and damp—damp like the rain I had once believed in praying for . . .

Heave! I threw myself against the dead weight of almost a ton of water. It didn't budge. Heave! *O God, help me! Someone help me!* Every ounce of strength was needed. Heave . . . something gave, pain ripped through my back, the tank lurched away as the wagon tipped up, and I was knocked spinning to the ground.

At first I thought I was sitting in a pool of blood but it was water sloshing from the tank. The wagon and tank lay crazily on their side. In a daze I saw that Carol's foot was unharmed except for a wide red bruise.

But the children were looking at me strangely, for I did not realize at first that I had been shouting.

I was suddenly looking at the sky, full face. My cheeks and dress were wet. "You hear!" I was shouting over and over, "There is a God! There is a God and He hears us . . ."

When my husband learned what had happened he could not believe that a lone woman had the strength to lift that huge steel tank full of water—and he was right. It took extra strength, and in the moment of my greatest need God gave me His strength.

A year has gone by. Spring already is behind us. The rain that began with such frequency in late April is still with us and the barrenness of the past summers is only a harsh memory. At times there is a pain in my side that was not there before, and now and then it makes a dull bid for attention. But when it does I smile to myself. It is a quiet reminder that no task is insurmountable, no loneliness unshared, and no sky empty— of God.

What on Earth *Is* Shoo-fly Pie, Anyway?

Mary Helen Livingston

he doctor closed his bag and turned to me. "Call me if he gets any worse this afternoon or tonight. I'll stop by in the morning to see him. If he's no better, I'll have to put him in the hospital. He needs fluids and he must eat."

"I've given him everything I can think of, but he just can't keep anything down."

"You must keep on trying. He is getting weak and dehydrated. Do your best. I'll see you tomorrow morning."

I sat down in the rocking chair by the sofa where my little

son lay. Bobby had always been thin and undersized; now, after days of battling an especially severe form of influenza, he looked wan and wasted. What would I do if he had to be hospitalized? I was a nursing student at Florida State University in Tallahassee and had no hospitalization insurance and very little money. What if the hospital refused to admit him? I prayed silently, "Lord, show me what to do."

"Bobby, suppose I go to the store and buy a different kind of soup for you. And maybe some Jell-O. Don't you think you might be able to eat some?"

"No, Mama."

"Can't you think of anything you'd like?"

"Make me some shoo-fly pie, Mama. I could eat that. I know I could."

Bobby had never eaten shoo-fly pie in his life. He could not desire something he had never seen or tasted. Yet I knew why he had asked. To pass the long, weary hours of illness, I had been reading stories to him from library books. *Yonie Wondernose* by Marguerite De Angeli was his favorite. It was the story of Johnny, a little Amish boy from the Pennsylvania Dutch area, and it described vividly the customs, dress, food, and daily activities of the Amish.

My life had been spent in Georgia and Florida. I knew nothing of the Amish, had never seen an Amish person, had never tasted a Pennsylvania Dutch dish. What on earth *is* shoo-fly pie anyway? A fruit pie? A custard pie? A savory meat concoction like shepherd's pie? The little story had mentioned shoo-fly pie, but had failed to list the ingredients. I doubted the wisdom of experimenting with strange, exotic foods in the middle of a serious illness. However, it was the only food Bobby had requested and maybe it was worth trying. Whatever was in it, it was probably not going to stay in him long enough to do any harm.

Having made the decision to act on Bobby's request, I set about locating a recipe. The Leon County Library did not have a book on Pennsylvania Dutch cookery, neither did the

State Library. The library at Florida State University had such a cookbook, but it was in use and not due back for two weeks. I called nearby bookstores. They had no Pennsylvania Dutch cookbooks. I called my neighbors, friends, relatives. Some of them had heard of shoo-fly pie; none of them knew what it was.

"Bobby, there isn't a recipe for shoo-fly pie in this town. I'm just as sorry as I can be. After you are well, we will try again, but right now we are going to have to do with what we can get. I'm going to the grocery store now and try to find something easy to eat for you. Your grandfather will sit with you while I'm gone."

"What store are you going to, Mama? I'll ask God to send you a recipe there. He'll send you one."

"Oh, no, Bobby," I said in alarm, "please don't do that!" I couldn't bear the thought of his faith being shattered. And there was obviously no way for God to provide a recipe in a grocery store. I had already tried all the likely places. It would be best for Bobby not to ask for the impossible.

"God will know how to send you a recipe, Mama. Are you going to Winn-Dixie?"

"Yes, I'm going to Winn-Dixie. Don't ask God, honey. I'll be back soon with something good."

In Winn-Dixie I pushed my shopping cart, filling it with red and green Jell-O, butterscotch pudding, chicken noodle soup. And then, nearing the checkout counter, I stood still, not believing what I saw. Walking in the door were two women, one wearing a black prayer cap, the other a white one, just like the pictures in *Yonie Wondemose*. Hurrying toward them, I asked, "Are you Amish?"

"Yes, we are Amish."

"And do you know how to make shoo-fly pie?"

"Of course. All Amish women know how to make shoo-fly pie."

"Could you write me a recipe?"

"Why, yes, certainly. If you have paper, I'll write it down

and then we will help you find the things you need to make a nice pie."

As we walked around gathering brown sugar, molasses, and spices, I asked them if they lived in Tallahassee.

"Oh, goodness, no! We are just passing through. We have been down in Florida and are on our way back home to Pennsylvania. I don't know why we stopped in here, but all of a sudden, my companion said, 'Let's stop at that Winn-Dixie.' So here we are. I really don't know why we came in."

Awestruck, humbled, and ashamed, I knew why. Bobby had disobeyed me. He had asked—and received.

When I walked into the living room with the groceries, Bobby said, "You got the recipe God sent, didn't you, Mama?"

The recipe made, not one, but two large shoo-fly pies. Bobby ate almost a whole pie during the late afternoon and early evening and drank several cups of weak tea. Moreover, he retained all he ate and drank. The pie, high in carbohydrates, provided energy, and the tea replaced lost body fluids. By morning, Bobby was able to drink fruit juices and eat poached eggs and toast. His improvement thereafter was rapid and dramatic.

And so, after all these years, there's a letter I want to write:

Dear Amish Ladies:

This story is really a long-overdue letter to you. It should have been written immediately after this incident, which happened so many years ago. I thought it was in 1954; Bobby says that it was 1955. His grandfather would remember exactly, but he died in 1976 and I cannot ask him. Please forgive me for not getting your names and addresses. How could I have been so preoccupied with my problems that I failed to provide myself with the means of thanking you two for the parts you played in this drama?

Perhaps, not knowing the beginning or end of the story, you regarded it as a trivial incident and pushed it away, into the vast storehouse of forgetfulness. I want to jog your memory. You had been

on a pleasure trip to Florida with friends and were driving back home.
You passed through the business district of Tallahassee, Florida. You
were driving north on Monroe Street, the highway to Thomasville,
Georgia, when you came to a Winn-Dixie on your right. Do you
remember?

I want you to remember because, to me, this was not a happen-
stance, a coincidence. Through the years, when my faith has faltered,
when cynicism has threatened me, I find myself thinking of a very sick
child making a simple request that he knew *would be granted.*
Unlike me, Bobby wasn't concerned with how *God was going to go*
about it; he trusted in His infinite power. It reminds me that I have
no right to wish my own human limitations on God, for with God
all things are possible. Thank you, dear Amish ladies, for being His
messengers.

AMISH SHOO-FLY PIE
(Yield: Two 8-inch pies)
Crumb Mixture
2 cups flour
¾ cup brown sugar
⅓ cup lard, shortening, or butter
½ teaspoon nutmeg ⎫
1 teaspoon cinnamon ⎭ optional

Mix above ingredients together thoroughly in a bowl until crumbs are
formed.
Syrup Mixture
1 cup molasses
½ cup brown sugar
2 eggs
1 cup hot water
1 teaspoon baking soda dissolved in hot water

In a separate bowl, mix syrup ingredients thoroughly. Pour half of the syrup mixture into unbaked pie-crust-lined 8-inch pie plate, then add half of crumb mixture; repeat with the other pie plate. Bake at 400 degrees F for 10 minutes, then reduce heat to 350 degrees F and continue baking for 50 minutes more. Cool before eating.

HER PLAYING DAYS WERE OVER
Philip K. March

*M*usic was like a second language to my mother. She learned to play the piano by ear, without lessons. She had perfect pitch, and her musicianship was so good she could transpose musical scores in her head. As a young woman she played the pipe organ for silent movies, craning her neck as she watched the films to interpret the antics of Buster Keaton or the fervor of Lillian Gish.

When I was a boy in Canton, Ohio, Mother often performed with our hometown symphony. Whenever famous violinists, cellists, oboists, or sopranos came to town on concert tours, my mother, Ruth, was the requested accompanist. And every Sunday for many decades she was a church organist.

My mother and father seemed to have an intuitive musical understanding between them. Mother told me how a song would run through her head as she worked in the kitchen while Dad, puttering in the basement, would hum the same tune—in the same key.

In her final years Mom lived in a nursing home. There was a piano in the activities room, but she never went near it. Severe arthritis had gnarled her fingers. Her playing days were over.

So it came as a surprise one evening when Mother asked to be taken to the activities room. The nurses wheeled her in. "Over to the piano," she whispered. They obeyed. Then my ninety-two-year-old mother put her hands to the keys for the first time in years, and she played. Beautifully.

That night, with the strains of Brahms and Chopin still echoing in the nursing home, Mother died in her sleep.

"She Couldn't Have Said a Word!"
Jeanne M. Dams

The hospital chaplain sat by the dying woman's bed in the hospice ward. He knew little about her, except that the end was near. She had fought bravely, but after her last operation the doctors said there was little that could be done. Now she was unconscious, and although he could not speak with her, he tried to find the right words of prayer.

Her bed was cranked up and she was half sitting, in order to make it easier for her to breathe through a tube in her throat. Her breaths came harshly and slowly, but their rhythm was even. In the warm room, the chaplain felt tired and closed his eyes for a minute.

Suddenly he was startled awake by a loud cry from the bed. The woman was sitting bolt upright. "My God!" she cried out.

The chaplain rose quickly to summon a nurse. But just then the woman sank back against the pillows, her eyes closed, a look of radiance on her face.

A nurse rushed in. "Did you call out?" she asked the chaplain as she took the woman's pulse. Quickly the nurse summed up the situation. "I'm afraid she's gone."

"No, I didn't speak," the chaplain said in wonderment, still thinking of the woman's ecstatic expression. "She did. She cried out, 'My God!' "

The nurse turned to him, puzzled. "But she couldn't have. Didn't you know? She had cancer of the larynx. Her voice box was destroyed weeks ago. She couldn't have said a word."

TRANSMISSION MISSION
Bill Steinfeldt

I loved my 1970 forest-green Chevy station wagon, and it was crucial to my family's new way of life. My wife, Lynette, four small kids, and I had recently moved from New York City to a tranquil country house parked by a friendly brook and guarded by big, old trees. But it put us temporarily in tight finances, and we just prayed the Chevy wouldn't break down. It was our only car.

I worked the 8:00 to 4:00 night shift as a policeman in the borough of Queens, fifty-five miles away. So when the Chevy's automatic transmission began to give me trouble after I'd scraped the bottom of the wagon on a curb during a rainstorm, I began to have a sick feeling inside. The transmission wouldn't kick out of first gear. My trip to the shop made me feel even worse. There, a man in a gray mechanic's jumpsuit gave me the cheerless news that the transmission was shot and would have to be replaced with a rebuilt one to the tune of one thousand dollars. My stomach turned over. He might as well have said one million.

At home that night I tossed and turned. Lynette suggested we pray about it, and I consented. But to tell the truth, I didn't really believe that I should be bothering God with life's everyday problems, even though our pastor, Cliff Avery, had preached that God cares about all of us, down to the smallest detail. Lynette and I had become good friends with Pastor Avery and his wife. In fact, they were coming for dinner the following Sunday after church.

"What are you going to do?" Lynette asked the next morning at breakfast.

"I have no choice," I said morosely. "I have to work."

Leaving three hours early, the Chevy and I crept in first gear, at twenty-five miles per hour, emergency flashers blinking, down the extreme right lane of the Merritt Parkway. Other drivers didn't exactly throw bouquets. At Shea Stadium, in Queens, where my police locker was, I changed into uniform, worked my tour of duty, and crept back home the same way.

After repeating the same routine for a week, I prayed again for help, but my faith was in the same low gear as my Chevy.

Sunday afternoon, as planned, Pastor Avery, his wife, and two young children came for dinner. I was bone tired from all the hassle with the car and still no solution in sight. At four o'clock I apologized for having to leave so early and explained my situation. Pastor Avery stood up. "Listen," he boomed in his strong, authoritative voice, "I have an idea. Let's all gather around your car. We pray for God to heal people in our church. Why can't we pray for Him to heal your car? I'd like to lay hands on it and pray."

I scratched my nose to cover a smile, but he was already headed for the door. Silently we all filed out and gathered around the green cripple glinting in the sunlight. His wife and mine and all six kids eagerly laid hands on the car. The pastor stood prominently at the hood, strong hands pressing down as if he expected it to rear up. I was behind him, in the shadow of a tree, eyeing the road and hoping we wouldn't be seen. I bowed my head politely and shoved my hands in my pockets.

"Lord, You know our brother's circumstances," he intoned in a voice that seemed to cover all of heaven and earth, not to mention the neighbor's yard. "Please heal this transmission. In Jesus' name, Amen."

They all watched as I started it up and backed it out. There was no change, but the pastor looked undaunted. I made my way to work.

At the end of the day I changed into civvies for the 4:00 A.M. trip home. *If only* . . . , I sighed as I slid behind the wheel. I turned the key and listened incredulously to *ummmm! . . . UMMMMM! . . . RUMMMM!* as I pulled out. The car was really moving . . . forty-five, fifty, fifty-five miles an hour! Remembering Pastor Avery's prayer, I felt goose bumps and pulled over and turned off the engine. This couldn't be happening! I started the car up again, gunned the motor, and got back on the road. I heard the same smooth cadence of gears changing from first to second to third.

I drove the Chevy without problems for another year, when I was able to get a newer car. I gave the Chevy to a poor family in our church. The husband drove it for several years till it had to be junked. "I hated to do it," he said, "because the motor and transmission still worked like a charm!"

Incidentally, it wasn't just the car that got out of first gear that long-ago day. So did my faith. I've been "bothering" God ever since with even the nittiest-grittiest things and finding out He really does care!

EASTER MORNING
Leroy Thomas

The stone wasn't rolled
    away from the tomb
So that Jesus could leave.
    He was already gone.

It was rolled away
    so that doubters like me
Could look in and cry,
    "I believe! I believe!"

Six

THE

SHINING

LIGHT

*S*uddenly a light from heaven flashed about him.

—*Acts 9:3,* RSV

"God is light," the Apostle John tells us (1 John 1:5). He is "the Father of lights" according to the Apostle James (1:17), the author and giver of good and perfect gifts. So it's no surprise to discover that He uses light and lights to communicate with us. The lights we read about in this section are of three kinds: the light of God's presence; lights mysteriously shining that point to God or that help people in trouble; and the light of love that, though unmeasurable by a light meter, still shows up on film, proving the truth of the psalmist's comment, "In thy light do we see light" (Psalm 36:9, RSV).

Why Were Our Landing Lights On?

G. H. Beaulaurier

On a cold January night I was captain of United Airlines flight 840 bound for San Francisco. We had taken off from Denver and had climbed to about twenty-nine thousand feet when a flight attendant knocked at the cockpit door. A passenger, she said, had just reported seeing a light flashing an SOS in the mountains beneath us. I no sooner got a fix on our position—sixty-two miles west of Denver on the J-60 airway—when the intercom chimed and another flight attendant told us of a second passenger who had seen the SOS signal.

Enough said. We called Air Traffic Control, advised them of the reports, and gave the estimated location. A commuter flight scheduled over that area was alerted to watch for the distress signal. The sheriff's office was apprised of the situation.

Not until we landed did we learn the whole story. Two people in a four-wheel-drive vehicle had ignored the "road closed due to snow" signs posted by the forest service and were trapped by an avalanche.

For two days and nights, they fought fatigue and frostbite. In desperation, they removed a headlight from the vehicle and rigged it to the battery so that they could send out SOS signals. Then they waited. But all the planes flying overhead were too high for them to see at night—until we came along.

And the only reason they were able to spot our jetliner was because our landing lights were on.

Our landing lights? To this day I do not know why those lights were on. Or do I?

<h2 style="text-align:center">SHELTER</h2>

Christine Brandenberger

*A*ll day long I had dreaded the thirty-mile drive. As a transplanted Californian, I wasn't used to the gray, unpredictable Aprils in Kansas. April 27 had been raw and drizzly, and at four o'clock, when I left to take the children to their cousin Stacey's birthday party, it was raining in earnest.

"Be extra careful," my husband, Bill, cautioned as Jennie, five, and Maria, three and a half, wrestled with their coats. I bundled our three-month-old baby, Will, into a satin sleeper. Bill wasn't coming with us because he needed time to study for upcoming medical-school exams.

The birthday party was worth the drive. My girls were impressed with Stacey's Holly Hobbie cake, and they were delighted to "help" play with Stacey's new doll. But when it was time to start for home, the sky was black and the rain torrential; the radio announced that fifty-mile-an-hour winds were buffeting the area. The dirt roads I'd come on would be nearly impassable, so Bill's father mapped out a route that would keep me on paved ones. I scooted the kids into our rattly '67 Plymouth.

I crept down the highway. I couldn't use my bright lights—the solid sheet of rain reflected them back in my face. With my dims, I could see only a few feet ahead. Somewhere I missed a turn and found myself on a gravel road. I turned at the next intersection, thinking I could backtrack to the highway.

I crept along mile after mile. The highway never appeared. I crossed a bridge—and the bottom seemed to fall out of the road. The car dropped, then bumped, and the wheels spun. I found myself on a dirt access road which curved along farm fields next to the riverbank. I shifted into low gear hoping for enough traction to pull myself out, but the car slipped sideways into a slough of mud. And stuck.

Wanting to save the battery, I switched off the lights and sat in the darkness, trying to calm my panic. The road I'd glimpsed in front of me was little more than a path, and it was highly unlikely anyone would be traveling on it before morning. Worse, the river might overflow if the rain continued. We would be swept away.

Lord, I prayed, *help me get the children out of here.*

The instant I looked up I spotted what appeared to be a yard light.

"There's a house just up the road," I told the girls. "We'll walk up there and call Daddy. I'll have to carry Will, so you both must hold tight to my coat pockets. The road will be filled with puddles, so whatever happens, don't let go."

The rain subsided to a drizzle just as we got out of the car. I was thankful for that, but the road was slick and uneven and we kept losing our footing. Worse, we'd only walked a few yards when, to my bewilderment, I realized the yard light I'd seen from the car had disappeared. I couldn't see anything at all.

The girls were afraid, and so was I! To reassure us, we sang "Jesus Loves Me" over and over again. But then Jennie stopped singing.

"If Jesus loves us, why isn't He down here with us?" she asked.

"Honey, it isn't Jesus' fault that Mommy got lost and stuck," I told her. "But Jesus really is with us, and He's showing me the way to go."

"But why isn't Jesus *walking* with us?" Jennie persisted.

All I could think of to say was, "He doesn't want to get His feet muddy."

Jennie and Maria giggled, but my fear was only relieved for a moment. Will was heavy—thirteen pounds—and my arms felt ready to drop off. The girls were dragging on my coat pockets, and I knew we couldn't go much farther.

A huge bolt of lightning split the sky, then hung suspended for several seconds, revealing a two-story white farmhouse. If the lightning had flashed twenty seconds later, we might have missed it completely.

We slogged our way onto the front porch, and I knocked on the door, first firmly, then more and more frantically. But the house was dark inside and no one answered. In desperation I tried the knob. Locked.

I sat the girls down on the steps and put Will in Jennie's arms.

"I'm going to the back door," I said. "The people who live here must be in bed, but I'm sure they'll wake up and let us in."

The back door was locked too. I beat on it until my hands hurt. I yelled until I was hoarse. No one came.

The rain started again, an incredible downpour, and the wind whipped it into a stinging frenzy. My children waited unprotected in the chilling gale.

Break into someone's home? *Never*. But I *had* to get into that house.

"Mommy!" Jennie screamed from the front porch. I could hear Maria crying.

I took a deep breath, doubled my fist and smashed it through the pane of glass alongside the back door. I reached in, pulled back the bolt, and flung the door open. Then I ran back around to the front, swept up the children and rushed them through the back door.

We held on to each other breathlessly, then looked around. An old floor lamp shone with just enough dim light for me to see the outlines of a stove . . . a refrigerator . . .

And . . . a telephone! Help was only a phone call away! I hurried to it.

The line was dead.

I put back the receiver and sank wearily against the wall. Will started to whimper. I flipped a light switch. Nothing. I tried another, then another. Nothing. Yet for some reason the single bulb of that dilapidated floor lamp gave forth a pale but steady light. Without it, we'd have been in total darkness.

The house didn't have much furniture, but there was a worn sofa covered in houndstooth-check nylon. I used the cushions to make a bed on the floor for the girls. When I pulled off their muddy slacks, I saw that Maria had walked right out of her little T-strap shoes somewhere on the muddy road and had continued barefoot. But she and Jennie had obeyed my instructions to hold on: my coat pockets were nearly ripped off.

"Mommy, are we safe now?" Jennie asked tiredly.

"Of course we are, darling," I said. Thank goodness she and her sister were too tired to detect the quiver of uneasiness in my voice. I was feeling anything but safe.

We had found shelter, but was that enough? True, there was a roof over our heads, and walls between us and the stormy blast. But my heart still beat anxiously. I had broken into the home of people I didn't know, damaged their property and used their possessions without permission. The walls around us kept out the wind and the rain, but my heart still beat uneasily. I was cold and feeling like the intruder I was.

A lightning flash illuminated the room, and my eyes fell on a small wooden plaque on a built-in hutch. I picked up the plaque and carried it to the kitchen lamp, where I read these words written in white:

The Lord Is My Shepherd.

A sense of peace enfolded me like two loving arms. This was a house where God-fearing people lived. And God was here. Now.

I lay down with my arms around the children, watching the play of lightning and listening to the wind, rain, and thunder. I was still worried about Bill and his parents. What would they think had happened to us? But I felt calm and secure for the first time in hours.

It must have been about 1:30 in the morning when I heard the click of a key in the front lock. I jumped up and hurried to the door and came face-to-face with a young man who looked as surprised as I was.

I poured out my story of why I was there, explaining that I'd never have broken in if I hadn't been desperate. "And," I ended breathlessly, "I knew, whoever you were, you'd be nice."

"Lady," he said, "I'm the owner of this house, and I hoped, whoever *you* were, that you'd be nice too."

The young man lived with his parents in town but was fixing up the house to live in after his upcoming marriage. He worked the late shift at a nearby plant, and on his way home had felt a strong urge to come by the house to see if the storm had done any damage.

He helped me carry the children to his car and took us to his parents' home, where I called my family. They had been frantically driving all over the countryside looking for us.

The next day, we returned to pay him for the damages and give him a plant as a small token of our thanks. He towed our car out with a tractor, and he even found little Maria's shoes in the mud. By that time his electricity, which had been knocked out by the storm, had been restored. He had no idea what yard light we could have seen, or why the dim kitchen light had continued to glow.

But he did know why the plaque was there. "Well, sure," he said matter-of-factly. "I put it there."

The Lord is my shepherd.

The young man's home was not just a shelter for us; it was a sanctuary.

THE LIGHT AND THE CROSS
Arthur Gordon

*I*n an airliner I found myself sitting next to a young woman who told me that she was a registered nurse. When she learned that I was a writer, she said, "I'll tell you a story, a true one. Maybe you can use it."

I smiled a little. "Maybe I can."

"Last week," she said, "I was on night duty. The patient in Room 78 was very frightened. Surgery was scheduled for the next morning and I knew the doctors did not give this woman much of a chance.

"I tried to cheer her and suggested that she pray for strength. She said she did not believe that prayers were answered, but I urged her to pray anyway.

"During the night I went into her darkened room with my

flashlight to see if she was all right. Then, rather suddenly, I was called away.

"In the morning a most extraordinary change had come over her. She no longer seemed frightened. 'I'm going to be all right,' she told me. 'I know, because I prayed, and my prayers were answered. I asked for a sign, and I was given one.'

"A sign?

" 'I saw a light,' she said in a whisper. 'And in the center of the light, a cross. It was on the wall at the foot of my bed. I'm going to be all right.'

"The attendants came then, and wheeled her away. When she was gone, I looked in the blankets at the foot of her bed and found what I was looking for—my flashlight. A week or so earlier I had dropped it, had cracked the glass, and had mended it with a tiny cross of adhesive tape. Obviously, when I came in during the night, I had left it by mistake. Half-buried in the blankets, it must have projected a circle of light, just as the patient said . . . with a cross in the center."

"And did the patient recover?"

"Of course she did! She thought her prayers were answered."

The nurse's voice died away. For a moment there was nothing but the drone of the engines.

"And what do you think?" I asked her.

The nurse smiled and shook her head. "I don't think," she said. "I know!"

The Light from Somewhere
Dicky Roth

The rain crashed like clouds of bullets on the cobbled streets of Oslo. Yet steadily more people joined the ranks, until they were eight-deep on each side of the road. And they were smiling.

"What's taking place?" I asked a man.

"It's Haakon's birthday," he said. "He'll ride through Oslo at two o'clock."

It was only noon, yet there they stood, surely everyone of Oslo's four hundred thousand, in the heavy deluge.

It was 1952 and I was making a colored film of Norway. The procession obviously would provide some fine shots. But in the rain there was barely enough light to see, let alone for color photography.

And yet I sensed a strange glow all around me. A soft light seemed to fill the streets. I searched everywhere but could not find its source. Puzzled, I took out my light-meter and measured the light; it registered nil. Still I knew there was a light, coming from somewhere.

Then, quite foolishly for a professional photographer who should know better, I reached for my cameras and started filming.

At last, at long wet last, the procession came out—one ordinary, everyday *open* car, one motorcycle cop at each side, a sound-car behind. That was all!

In the back seat of the open car an elderly man sat alone. As he approached, an immense sound arose from the people.

It started as a mighty cheer, then seemed to stumble: four hundred thousand lumps in four hundred thousand throats. One got into mine, too, as I looked at that kindly figure, erect and smiling, with the rain beating him mercilessly.

I ground my camera and then dashed ahead in my car. I reached the big hospital ahead of the procession and there, to my horror, on the pavement in the pouring rain, in beds, wheelchairs, stretchers, I found the sick, the lame, the halt— umbrellas held over them, carefully covered up with hospital rubber sheeting, nurses and doctors standing behind them— all smiling radiantly.

I cried out, impulsively, "Oh, dear people, you mustn't wait out here! There's nothing to see. There's only one car with one man in it."

They all looked at me compassionately, their bright smiles never leaving their rain-spattered faces. Then one man spoke:

"Thank you," he said in English, "but, you see, that one man is Haakon, today is his eightieth birthday. And it is not only that we want to see *him,* we want *him* to see *us*. Each of us wants Haakon to know that today we wish him well."

As I listened to him other things I'd heard came back to me . . . The tailor, fitting my new coat, who had chatted of the Oslo Rotary Club where the King drops in informally. "Haakon is the head both of our government and our Norwegian Lutheran Church. He likes to know about all of our problems . . ." The bus driver who talked about the German invasion and Haakon's refusal to replace the Norwegian cabinet with Nazi-picked men. Escaping the German purge, Haakon removed his government to England where he kept up the fight. I remembered, too, that Norwegians never say "The day the war ended," but "The day Haakon came home . . ."

Just then the car with Haakon in it drove past. Up went the most robust cheer I ever heard—from wheelchairs, beds, and stretchers. He waved to them and was gone. The cheer quieted into a collective, tender sigh.

When, at 6:30 that evening in the pouring rain, Haakon spoke from the balcony of the Town Hall, I was there with my cameras. And as the crowds still danced in the streets at eleven o'clock, I was still, idiotically, filming in the dark.

Next day I stacked up all the film I'd used and wasted. Weeks later, when they came back to me, processed, I tossed them aside without troubling to examine them. I knew they would be blank.

But one day, tidying up my workshop before throwing the whole pack out, I half-heartedly put one roll of "Haakon's Birthday" on the projector. I gasped! It had all come out—in color!

Stunned, I reran the film, again and again. Everything I had photographed was there: the rain, the people, Haakon. Despite the dark day, the scenes were vividly clear and colorful. Suddenly, I discovered where the precious light originated. It was in the people's eyes as they looked fondly at their leader—the man whose own devout goodness and dedication had aroused in them a deep devotion. Studying their faces on the screen, I realized that on a dark day in Oslo I had filmed King Haakon's birthday procession by the light of pure *love!*

LOVE
William Blake
from The Clod and the Pebble

Love seeketh not itself to please,
Nor for itself hath any care,
But for another gives its ease,
And builds a Heaven in Hell's despair.

A Strange Soft Light
Malcolm Muggeridge

*A*fter the experience of interviewing Mother Teresa, I had a consuming desire to go to Calcutta and participate in making a television program about her and her work. This became possible in the spring of 1969, thanks to the British Broadcasting Company. Our cameraman was Ken Macmillan, who covered himself with glory filming the Kenneth Clark series, *Civilisation.*

We arrived at Calcutta airport on one of those heavy, humid days for which Bengal is famous. The air seems to distill into water as one breathes it, and every movement costs one a stupendous effort. A general strike, we were told, had been organized for the following day. As we only had five days to do our filming, we decided to go almost at once to 54A Lower Circular Road, the address of the Missionaries of Charity. Mother Teresa was waiting for us in the little courtyard of their house. The sight of her, or even the thought of her, always gives me a great feeling of happiness.

The filming began. It is not just my opinion, but that of all concerned, that it proceeded with quite exceptional smoothness and speed: our next move always seemed to be obvious; there were none of the usual breakdowns and crises. Above all, there was no bickering or quarreling, which, in the circumstances of filmmaking, is almost unavoidable. In the ordinary way, making a fifty-minute documentary, which is what our film came out at, takes two to three months. To produce a sufficiency of footage in five days necessarily put a heavy

strain on all concerned; it was impossible to get a report on
the film taken before moving elsewhere, so there was no
chance of redoing any that was unsatisfactory. As it turned
out, all was well.

All this amounted to a kind of miracle. There was another
actual miracle. Part of the work of the sisters is to pick up the
dying from the streets and bring them into a building given
to Mother Teresa (a sometime temple dedicated to the cult of
the goddess Kali), there, as she puts it, to die within sight of
a loving face. Some do die; others survive and are cared for.

This Home for the Dying is dimly lit by small, high windows and Ken was adamant that filming was quite impossible
there. We could not get the place adequately lighted in the
time at our disposal. It was decided that, nonetheless, Ken
should have a go, but by way of insurance he took, as well,
some film in an outside courtyard.

In the processed film, the part taken inside was bathed in
a particularly beautiful soft light, whereas the part taken outside was rather dim and confused.

How to account for this? Ken has all along insisted that,
technically speaking, the result is impossible. To prove the
point, he used some of the same stock in a similarly poor light,
with completely negative results. I am absolutely convinced
that the technically unaccountable light is, in fact, the "Kindly
Light" Newman refers to in his well-known exquisite hymn.

Mother Teresa's Home for the Dying is overflowing with
love, as one senses immediately on entering it. This love is
luminous, like the halos artists have seen and made visible
round the heads of the saints. I find it not at all surprising that
the luminosity should register on a photographic film. The
supernatural is only an infinite projection of the natural, as the
furthest horizon is an image of eternity.

One thing everyone who has seen the film seems to be
agreed about is that the light in the Home for the Dying is
quite exceptionally lovely. This is, from every point of view,
highly appropriate. Dying derelicts from the streets might

normally be supposed to be somewhat repellent, giving off stenches, emitting strange groans. Actually, if the Home for the Dying were piled high with flowers and resounding with musical chants—as it may well have been in its Kali days—it could not be more restful and serene. So the light conveys perfectly what the place is really like: an outward and visible luminosity manifesting God's inward and invisible present love. This is precisely what miracles are for—to reveal the inner reality of God's outward creation.

A Narrow Window

Florence Earle Coates

A narrow window may let in the light,
A tiny star dispel the gloom of night,
A little deed a mighty wrong set right.

A rose, abloom, may make a desert fair;
A single cloud may darken all the air;
A spark may kindle ruin and despair.

A smile and there may be an end to strife;
A look of love, and hate may sheathe the knife;
A word—ah, it may be a word of life!

A Friend Was in Danger
Margaret Mackay

A fter World War II, I made a close friend in Alicia, an American living in London, who had been a very brave Red Cross girl in the Pacific. On a volunteer job in the tropics, she had picked up one of those grim diseases which are slow in developing. She had married, with outstanding happiness, before she found that the germ was insidiously eating away her strength.

Then she put up a heroic fight to keep her marriage and her home going. When the doctors said that most other people would have been dead, she set out to regain her health, by courage—and by faith. She stayed up most of the time, dragging about gamely, but every now and then she would have a spell which would keep her in bed for weeks, in pain and fever and attrition.

Oddly enough, wherever I might be, and even though we might not write to each other for weeks, I always seemed to feel it in my bones when she was having one of her attacks. Then I would send her a cheerful letter by special delivery, or a light, irrelevant telegram.

One November day I was down in Italy when I sensed— out of nowhere, like an odor—that she was very ill indeed. I sent off a nonchalant telegram about missing her in Rome and hoping to see her at Christmas time. Then, though I had no answer, I wrote every two or three days for several weeks. I carried the sensation of her need with me like a drop of cologne on my handkerchief, so that I was poignantly aware of her wherever I went.

I do not happen to be a Catholic, but I love to go into the old Roman churches with their rich residue of the countless prayers that have gone up like incense, and the contact with the innumerable people who have said them in sorrow and hope and gratitude. During those weeks, I often lit a candle and put a few lire in the box for the poor, and also for Alicia.

In Italian towns there are little shrines on many street corners: majolica plaques built into the masonry above the cobblestones, with a lamp flickering; or painted and lighted figures of the Madonna and Child. And whenever I saw these—hundreds of them, as I returned northward through Italy and up into Switzerland—I would pause and think a prayer for Alicia.

In Switzerland, my bedroom window looked out into an Alpine snow scene, with white-frosted fir trees and the spire of a small Gothic church. Above the church door, in a niche curtained with hanging snow, was a miniature shrine, with a stone-carved Madonna, simple and touching as a country doll. A little lamp was kept burning underneath.

Whenever I went to the window, there was the shrine; and there, for me, was Alicia. One night I could not sleep. I got out of bed and crept shivering to the window. In the snowy stillness, with not even a star in the hushed dark, the tiny lamp was burning steadily. I put all my heart into the thought of it then, for I sensed somehow that Alicia had reached her crisis.

And as it turned out—she had. A few days later, I had a note from her husband, telling me that she had been very ill for weeks and was just starting to recover from the worst attack of all.

When I got back to London before the holidays, I found her pale and bony, but nevertheless up on her feet and struggling to make a vivid Christmas for her Charlie—who adored her, as well he might.

"I was really very critically ill this time," she told me, while we sat on a sofa before the fire. "Charlie says I was delirious. He says I kept babling about a little shrine. And one night, when my fever was very high, and I was in desperate pain—I can't recall anything else out of the blur of misery, but one thing stays with me distinctly. I can remember seeing a dark scene, and a tiny lamp burning, and—clear as if it was right before my eyes—a Madonna and Child in a little shrine."

SEEING THE LIGHT
Virginia Sendor

*I*n the late 1970s a chain of deaths—my mother's, a younger brother's, a close aunt's—left me utterly grief-stricken and despairing. If only I had used my time with Mama more wisely during her last days! Did she and Richard and Aunt Julia ever know how much I really loved them? Was there anything they had wanted to tell me before they died, but I never gave them a chance?

Despite my professional background in rehabilitation counseling, I was haunted by painful feelings and questions. I decided to enroll in a graduate workshop on "Counseling for Death, Dying and Bereavement" at Hofstra University in Hempstead, New York. And it was in that class, on a frosty January morning in 1981, that I came to terms with a mysterious event in my life.

The professor began talking, in a matter-of-fact voice,

about something she called "near-death experiences." Such experiences, she stressed, were so well documented that there was even a worldwide group devoted to them called the International Association for Near-Death Studies, Inc.

My thoughts whirled. Could this professor be talking about the same sort of experience I'd had twenty-one years before? An experience so real, yet so bizarre, that I'd never told a soul about it? A rush of long-held-back memories flooded my mind. It seemed like yesterday.

It was spring, 1960. I'd learned to live with a severe hearing impairment that had affected me since childhood, and I'd even earned a master's degree in special education, majoring in rehabilitation counseling. But I was very ill. The news from my doctor was devastating: acute uremic poisoning with complications. He said I had three to six months to live.

At first I didn't have the courage to reveal this prognosis to my husband, Bernie. When I told my mother, she urged that I be treated at a special clinic in Texas run by a doctor she trusted. She offered to help take care of my children, three and six, while I was away. So I traveled to Dr. Herbert Shelton's clinic in San Antonio, Texas. Mama and Dad took the children, and since money was tight, Bernie stayed home to work.

The clinic, in an isolated area far from the downtown and residential areas of San Antonio, was surrounded by the scrubby Texas brushland and mile upon mile of open sky. I fully expected to die there. After about three months of following a strict vegetarian diet and drinking nothing but pure water and juices, I seemed to be getting worse. I was very weak. The thought of dying frightened me, but I was so ill that I almost began to welcome death to be free from pain.

And then, on a clear September day, the most extraordinary thing happened. I left my body on the bed and was hovering up by the ceiling of my room. And then—I was outside the building. I had no more pain and was no longer

aware of my body. Below me and around me was a pano-
ramic view of the vast Texas landscape and the horizon. I
seemed to be at one with the universe. I had no sense of time
or space.

Next I became aware of sounds that I hadn't been able to
hear without my hearing aid since I was a little girl. And what
I heard was the most beautiful music—an ethereal blend of
sounds, so natural as to surround me, envelop me. In addition
to the music, I heard some words—the same phrase chanted
over and over again. I didn't know the language, yet it was
strangely familiar.

I floated and seemed to be beyond the horizon, and then
in the distance appeared the graceful profile of a being with
shoulder-length hair. It was a blazing silhouette from the
waist up and glowing with its own most beautiful brilliant-
white light. Like the music, this light seemed to surround me,
envelop me, shine right through me. Although it was white,
it seemed to possess all the colors of the rainbow, like the light
that radiates from a perfectly cut diamond.

I was filled with a sense of wholeness and peace unlike
anything I'd ever known. "The Light" I experienced was
love, pure and unconditional—the "something more" that
I'd yearned for since I was a child.

Now, with crystal clarity, came these words: *"Baruch Atah
Adonai . . . Baruch Atah Adonai."* They were woven like a
golden thread through the beautiful music that surrounded
me. *". . . Baruch Atah Adonai."* I had no idea what the words
meant.

Then I was back in my room again, in my bed. I felt weak
and racked with pain. My chest felt crushed. I couldn't
breathe. And there was something terribly wrong with my
left side. Dr. Shelton and some attendants crowded around
my bed.

Later on I learned I had suffered an angina attack, but I
would be all right. My left side was palsied, but months of
intensive physical therapy enabled me to regain the use of my

arm and leg; gradually my overall health improved. Three months later, in December 1960, I was able to go home.

Though I am Jewish, I wasn't brought up in a religious home. Nevertheless I sensed that I had undergone a deeply spiritual experience. Something too meaningful to risk being ridiculed or diminished in any way. So I told no one, not even Bernie, about "The Light." I felt protective. The experience was too deeply personal to be shared at that time.

Then, twenty-one years later, while sitting in a college classroom with the nurturing support of about twelve of my peers, I felt a powerful sense of affirmation; I began to see a connection between the deaths that had led me to attend this class and my own near-death experience. It was an awakening.

I completed the course and plunged into advanced studies on death, dying, and bereavement. Meanwhile, I solved the puzzle of those words I'd heard. They had sounded vaguely familiar, like Hebrew, so I made an appointment with the rabbi of our local synagogue.

I met with him several days later in his paneled office and told him about my experience and the words. I was sharing what happened for the first time—and I felt as if it had just occurred. "Rabbi," I said, "it was many years ago that I heard those words. What do they mean?"

He looked at me intently. *"Baruch Atah Adonai,"* repeated the rabbi softly, stroking his chin, "means 'Blessed art Thou, O Lord.' " I gasped and repeated, *"Baruch Atah Adonai—* Blessed art Thou, O Lord." How appropriate!

Blessed art Thou, O Lord. So many nights as I drifted off to sleep, dog-tired from studying, I felt my strength and well-being restored as I recalled the magnificent "Light," the beautiful music, the reverent words.

Over the next year, I found myself increasingly drawn toward the study and practice of hospice care and counseling to help terminally ill patients and their loved ones. At the heart of hospice philosophy is understanding death as a natural part of life; an experience not to be shied away from or denied, but met with confidence and hope. The idea is to improve the quality of the life remaining to the patient and not to prolong the dying process.

Recalling Mama's, Richard's, and Aunt Julia's drawn-out battles with cancer, I understood the hospice belief that, while pain control is always necessary, in some cases a course of radical surgery or the use of heroic measures *or* extended therapy with drugs, chemicals, and radiation, may not be the best use of the time the dying patient has left.

Healing can occur on many levels, and it may not always mean a physical cure. The dying person is often in need of deep emotional and spiritual healing as well. And so is the family. "You can't learn everything about hospice work from books," explained a dear friend who is a clinical-oncology nurse specialist. "You need to be able to listen at a different level, intuitively, so you can respond to the unspoken needs of dying patients and their families and friends."

Listen at a different level. That was one thing I knew I could do after nearly half a century of living with a severe hearing loss. Many times I'd watched a person say one thing with his lips, while his eyes and face and body communicated an altogether different message.

On Christmas day, 1981, I was nearing the end of a double shift as a volunteer in the hospice unit of one of our local hospitals. One of the patients was a middle-aged man dying of cancer; he had been hospitalized for a period of time and had become comatose.

The medical community generally agrees that, even when comatose, the patient is aware—however dimly and mysteriously—of the presence of others, aware not only of their presence, but also aware of what they are saying and doing. I explained this to the man's wife and two grown daughters as they stood in painful silence outside his room.

"He knows you're here," I said. "He knows it's Christmas

day. Come into the room. Say his name. Talk to him. Share your love for him. He *will* hear you." I asked his wife, her face drawn with exhaustion and grief, to stroke her husband's cheek. "Kiss his forehead," I whispered.

Death was imminent, and the man's extremities were cold and turning blue. I asked one of the daughters to take her father's hand into her own. "Hold it tightly with both of your hands," I said.

I asked the other daughter to cradle her father's feet. "Cup them in your hands and massage them gently," I said. "Stroke his toes, his ankle . . . There, give him some of your warmth and life . . ."

Then I stepped aside, over to the window. I joined the family in my mind and spirit, praying that healing would take place where it was needed, in whatever form that might be.

I saw the man's toes start to move just the tiniest bit. And then a bit more. His color began improving.

"Look!" exclaimed the daughter at his side. "He's beginning to move!"

Then the man's eyes opened wide. He was not disoriented in any way, as might be expected considering his critical condition. Clear and bright, his eyes shone with joy, reflecting love. He was aware of all that was going on around him.

Before leaving the room to allow the family time alone, I encouraged them to share their deepest feelings with him. "Now is your chance to complete any unfinished business you may have with one another. Now is the time to talk about love—to say words you always wanted to say but never had time to—or to ask forgiveness."

As I left, I realized that my own pain about Mama, Richard, and Aunt Julia had been eased by helping this family.

And when I returned some three-quarters of an hour later, I saw something that took my breath away. For present in that patient's room were not only the patient and his family—*but "The Light" was there too!* Filling the room with a glorious radiance, shining in our eyes, *"The Light" was with us!*

My hospice work has taught me that in this life, along with the joy, are pain, sorrow, suffering, death. But through it all, God cares. He is light—*"The* Light." And when God's Light breaks through our darkness, it is with a power strong enough to redeem even the most hopeless-seeming situation—even death itself. To me death is not hopeless. It is not the end.

Baruch Atah Adonai!

WHEN THE CROSS SHONE
Ron Slaughter

In late winter 1970, Bud and Jane Surber helped erect a large cross on a hill near their home as part of a 4-H Club project. "We got it up and lit just in time for Easter," Jane Surber recalls. For a while its huge beams were illuminated by eight-foot-long fluorescent tubes, but in time it fell into disrepair, the electrical wiring failed, and the lights on the cross went out.

Nearly twenty years passed. In October 1989 the Surbers' son-in-law died and they wanted to make the cross shine again as a memorial to him. So Bud Surber climbed the hill to see if he could fix it. A skilled electrician, he worked on the cross for several days, but he was unable to get the lights back in working order. The cross remained dark.

But when winter arrived, something strange happened. One night the lights on the cross went on again, seemingly of their own accord. No one knew why. Truckers who passed the cross on U.S. 285 near Salida, Colorado, found it shining on the hill. Families hurrying to worship services could see it from their car windows.

That night the Surbers felt especially warmed by the cross's glow, for of all nights, that night was best. That night was Christmas Eve.

PART TWO

When
God
Works

Seven

WHEN

WE

FEEL

SEPARATED

And Jesus came and said to them, ". . . I am with you always, to the close of the age."

—Matthew 28:18, 20, RSV

Distance and death are the great separators in our lives. Yet the Apostle Paul tells us that nothing can separate us from the love of God in Jesus Christ—no measurement of any distance, and not even death (Romans 8:38–39). So it is that our feelings of grief and separation often open us up to experience God's presence and love in special and mysterious ways.

A PLACE AT THE TABLE

Peggy Eastman

T he fourteen-pound turkey sat ready for the oven. On the night before Thanksgiving, the plates were already stacked—eleven of them—and the knives, forks, and spoons were laid out neatly on the white lace tablecloth. I mentally ticked off the serving dishes and counted the glasses and napkins—cloth ones I'd have to wash and iron. But this was a special Thanksgiving, and paper napkins just wouldn't do.

My life was settling down after the loss of my husband in a plane crash four years earlier. The emotional scars were healing. I'd just become engaged, and I was looking forward to giving thanks for my new fiancé, Rudy. I'd even written down a short blessing to say: "Dear Lord, on this Thanksgiving Day, let us bless Your name without ceasing, for we know that all things good and lovely and loving come from You. Amen."

As I stood at the sink scrubbing pans, I began to feel chills. *Just tired,* I thought, continuing to work. The chills did not let up. I put on a sweater, turned up the heat. The chills got worse. My teeth were chattering and now my throat was sore. My head felt hot. All of a sudden I felt so tired I could no longer stand up. *Oh, no, not the flu. Not now. Not when I've planned everything and counted on having everyone here.*

I dragged myself up the stairs and crawled under the quilt on my bed, fully clothed except for my shoes. But the chills wouldn't stop. Finally I picked up the phone and, with a wobbly voice, called off my special Thanksgiving dinner. "No visitors," I told my mother. "I'll just have to stay in bed and get over this." We arranged to have the turkey picked up; my sister-in-law would have the dinner. My fiancé, a widower, would have dinner with his children. A wave of sadness swept over me. My plates, glasses, and serving dishes would go unused. God would go unthanked in this silent house.

Thanksgiving day I lay in bed with my golf ball throat and my fever, alone in the house except for my dog. I reached down and stroked her thick black fur, then let her out. Tired and out of breath just from negotiating the stairs, I settled back on my pillow.

Some Thanksgiving. We were supposed to thank God for our afflictions as well as our joys, but I didn't feel like thanking Him for the flu. I tried to remember what our prayer leader had said in church about coming closer to God when you least felt like it. She'd said, "You have to practice the presence of God. Pray as you can; don't pray as you can't."

Still angry and full of self-pity, I closed my eyes and tried to pray silently, willing my mind to center on God. But my mind rebelled. I thought about how I would have to take off the white lace cloth, put away the plates and serving dishes. I thought about the wash. About buying dog food. I thought about myself, and how awful the flu made me feel.

I tried again. I asked God to help me set aside my anger and self-pity. *Lord, I may be sick in bed but I don't have the spiritual flu; please help me come closer to You.* My mind quieted. One by one I visualized the faces of those dear to me who would be celebrating Thanksgiving without me. I thanked God for them. But I yearned to be with them.

I lost all sense of time and space as my mind free-floated in prayer. My bedroom with its patchwork quilt and embroidered blue bouquet of flowers on the wall faded from my consciousness. I was not aware of breathing, of being sick. I was not aware of being.

Later, I don't know how much later, the phone rang. "It

was the strangest thing," my mother was saying. My sister-in-law, she said, had miscounted and set out an extra plate. "We all felt, well, almost as if another person were here.

"And then—all of a sudden a blessing just seemed to come to me and I said it at the table," said my mother. "I really hadn't planned it; you know how we always hold hands and say the family grace."

"Do you remember the blessing you said?" I asked quietly.

"Dear Lord," said my mother into the telephone, "let us bless Your name without ceasing, for we know that all things good and lovely and loving come from You."

"Amen," I said.

"MOM, MOM!"
Carol L. Mackay

When the girls were young I could hear them calling for me at night, "Mom, Mom!" if they were sick or troubled, and I would go rushing down the hall to their bedsides. But this time when I heard the cry "Mom, Mom!" both daughters were grown, and Kathryn was a married woman, traveling halfway around the world with her husband, Peter. Still, it was unmistakable—she was calling me.

Picking up a Bible from the nightstand, I went into the family room to pray. I had a feeling of great urgency; Kathy needed help. "Dear God, show me what to do," I prayed. Then I turned to the 91st Psalm, repeating it over and over again, before I was able to feel at peace.

A few weeks later we got a letter postmarked from Singapore. "I'm grateful to be able to write this," Kathy began. "I can now tell you I was quite ill in Borneo with some sort of flu. We were there, doing our usual exploring one afternoon, when I suddenly became very sick and feverish.

"Back in our room, Peter became worried. As I rambled incoherently, he searched for someone who knew of a good doctor. Finally he found a local doctor who came to our scruffy, rented room. Seeing our predicament, this good man invited us to his house, where he and his housekeeper nursed me back to health—thank God."

What touched me most came at the end of the letter. "Remember when I was a girl, and I would call out, 'Mom,' and you would come rushing down the hall? That night in Borneo, in my fever, I called . . .

"And then I could hear you rushing down the hall."

ALWAYS A DREAM
Constance Foster

My Uncle Bill flew an old crate in World War I, and loved every moment in the air over France. In his pocket he carried pictures of his wife and the baby son he had never seen; at night he dreamed about going home to them.

He had other dreams, too, about making this world safe for democracy. He remembered how Jane had said of him on their honeymoon, "Always a dreamer . . ." and smiled. Anyway, they were fine dreams he had of freeing people and making the world a better place for the little fellows like himself to live in. The trouble was, when he'd been back home for a while, Jane protested; he didn't do anything about making a better place for his own little fellow, Chuck, to live in.

"Just look at that backyard," she groaned, "a regular pigsty; Chuck doesn't have a decent place to play."

But my Uncle Bill and my cousin Chuck thought that the yard was a wonderful place. It was full of old wooden packing boxes they could use for make-believe airplanes to fly around the world together. Bill had placed a small one for a cockpit on top of a large one and rigged up two boards for wings.

"Look, Chuck, there's Afghanistan down there under us," Bill would point out to the four-year-old. Or, "We're right over Egypt now. See the Nile flowing along like a green satin ribbon?"

Sometimes Bill let Chuck take the stick alone. At four, Chuck was a rather timid little boy, clamoring earnestly, "You won't let me crack up, will you, Daddy? You'll help me out if I get in a jam?"

"Of course I won't let you crack up, Son," his father assured him gravely. "You can always count on me no matter when or where."

Chuck believed it with all his heart, but nobody else figured that Bill was a man to be counted on. He held half a dozen jobs briefly and dreamed his way right out of them. Folks said he was impractical—a good man but a daydreamer. Jane had to go back to teaching school in order to support the family.

"Chuck thinks you're a hero now," she said to Bill one day. "But what will he think of you later when he finds that you can't hold even a mediocre job without fluffing it?"

That bothered Bill, for he knew it was true. Chuck was growing older now, also growing smarter. He'd soon see his dad for what he really was—only a dreamer.

So one day Bill put his toothbrush in his pocket and left town. Now and then, a postcard would come from South America or the Orient. Chuck saved every one of them; he loved the strange foreign stamps, and the adventure his father represented. He thought more of him than ever, now that he was off on a glamorous crusade of action. Then word came that Bill had joined up with the Loyalists in Spain and was flying a fighter. Chuck's heart swelled with pride. He was eighteen now, a husky six-footer.

Bill was a fool for luck—or maybe his son's prayers had something to do with it. He came through his second war without a scratch. But the old ticker was showing the combined effects of his added years and steady neglect of himself.

It wasn't until Chuck enlisted in the Air Force after Pearl Harbor that Bill came home to stay. The boy wanted it that way. Jane knew he'd been praying about a private dream of his own—having his father and mother together again. She was older now, so was Bill. The old complaints no longer mattered so much. Her teacher's pension would take care of their simple needs.

She and Bill lived for the boy's letters after he left to fly a bomber in the South Pacific. They enjoyed a new closeness that next year. Bill hadn't changed much, except to get grayer and shorter of breath. But Jane found comfort in taking care of him.

But neither of them was really living, there in the old house. They were living out on the vast expanse of the shining South Pacific. That was when they took to praying together. Maybe they were powerless, but God wasn't.

Chuck told me later about the thing that happened out there on a blazing hot day. He said he was thinking about the folks at home when he took off from the carrier on a routine bombing mission.

"It's yesterday—May 5th—back there in Centerville," he figured as he glanced at his wrist watch. "It must be about 8:00 P.M. They've finished supper and probably Dad's watering the lawn while Mom cleans up in the kitchen."

It was on the return trip that he ran into trouble. Somehow he was separated from the rest of the formation, and three enemy planes jumped on him. Their bullets killed his gunner and crippled his plane. Chuck felt his right arm go dead, and blood poured from a wound in his shoulder. Suddenly he began to black out. His head whirled. The last thing he remembered was that his father suddenly seemed to be sitting right there beside him in the cockpit. In a quiet, steady voice he was telling him just what to do.

"I won't let you crack up, Son, I promised, remember? You're going to make it back to the carrier, just hold on. Ease back on your stick—a little more altitude. I have my hand on that artery. And God is here with us, too, Chuck. He's always with us wherever we are."

Chuck heard it all through a black haze. But he was doing what Bill said, holding the plane on course.

"You're a great flyer, Dad. The best."

"Just a dreamer, Chuck," the older man chuckled. "But they've been good dreams."

Somehow Chuck set the plane down on the carrier, and they lifted him out. He was unconscious from loss of blood. It was several weeks before mail from the States reached him in his hospital bed. His mother had written the letter. Chuck still has it.

"Dad had seemed so much better lately," she told him. "He'd had a heart attack, but the doctor said he was going to get over it. I went upstairs to give him his medicine at 8:00 P.M., but he was asleep. I wasn't going to rouse him, but just as I was tip-toeing out of the room he sat bolt upright in bed and said, 'Chuck needs me. I've got to go to him, Jane, I promised.' I gave him his pill and told him he'd been dreaming. 'Always a dreamer, eh?' he smiled as I tucked him in.

When I came back an hour later he was lying there still smiling. But he was dead."

Bill had slipped away between 8:00 and 9:00 P.M. on the evening of May 5 when it was already tomorrow out on the South Pacific, out where Chuck was in such dire need of a good flyer like his dad.

THE SIGN
William Schmitz

I was on a hunting trip that gray September afternoon when the word came that Frank was dead. Frank, our twenty-year-old son, the baby of our family. I was stunned. I wanted to scream that it couldn't be true.

But it was true. Frank had been killed instantly when the small plane he was flying had gone into a spin and crashed.

All the time during that long trip home, through my tears, I relived in my mind Frank's short life. So much had been crowded into it.

One day when he was thirteen, I found him lying in the street unconscious from multiple injuries from a motor-scooter accident. He spent weeks in the hospital recovering from a skull fracture. During that time Frank had developed a deep personal relationship with God.

As Frank recovered at home, we'd catch him studying the sports pages longingly. He'd been a star baseball and football player in school, but now his damaged body seemed to rule that out. When he was finally able to limp about, he craved exercise and I built a set of outdoor high bars for him.

After the funeral, our two older sons returned to their homes and my wife, Polly, and I were alone in our grief. I tried to go back to my work as a petroleum geologist but it was useless. I'd sit in my office, turning a pencil over and over in my hand asking, *Why? . . . why?*

I couldn't seem to do anything any more except think about Frank. "O God," I cried, "please give us some sign . . . some acknowledgment that he is safe with You."

But Polly and I sank deeper into our depression. One Sunday, however, we took a drive. When we returned home and I reached to turn off the ignition, Polly stiffened and clutched my arm. "Bill, look!" she gasped. She pointed to the earth below the high bars.

I could not believe what I saw. There glowing in the late afternoon sun stood two blood-red lilies in a place where nothing had ever grown before. They grew straight and sturdy from the earth in the same spots Frank had placed his feet to exercise.

Polly and I marveled how they got there. The area had been mowed only a day earlier. We had once placed a swing on the high bar for our grandchildren and the trampled earth was like iron. But there they stood.

The lilies flourished for two weeks. Then they were gone.

But we didn't need them any more to assure us that Frank was safe with Him.

God's Footprint
Bliss Carman
from Vestigia

I took a day to search for God,
And found Him not. But as I trod
   By rocky ledge, through woods untamed,
   Just where one scarlet lily flamed,
I saw His footprint in the sod.

"Tell Mary to Wait"
Beverly Fowler

My father was one of eight children. His mother suffered a breakdown after the eighth child was born and was absent during their formative years. My father was five at the time and his seven-year-old sister, Mary, became "Little Mother" to him. A closeness developed between them that lasted all their lives.

As a girl I knew there was something special about that closeness. On certain Sundays after church, Dad would decide unexpectedly to drive to Mary's house, fifty miles away. Mother always felt Dad should let her know first, but Dad would say, "No, Mary's expecting us." Sure enough, when we arrived, the table would be set for guests and a child's chair would be ready for me. "I knew you were coming," Mary would say.

In old age, Aunt Mary retired to Florida and Dad moved to a retirement home near us in Pennsylvania. One day, though he had not spoken to her in months, Dad announced sadly, "Mary's gone." It was so. Mary had died that very morning.

One morning two years later we gathered around my father's hospital bed. We knew he had only hours to live. He looked at my mother and asked, "Is Mary still here?"

Mother was startled, and answered, "I don't know, dear."

"She was here all night." He gestured toward the head of his bed. "Tell her to wait." Those were his last words.

Of course we knew that Mary had not been there that night, but we were comforted by the thought that, close as they were, Mary would indeed be waiting for him. That would be so like her.

GLORIA'S PROMISE
Nikki McFaul

T he first time I saw Gloria Marshall she was singing in the choir at Fairview Community Church, here in Costa Mesa, California. My six-year-old son, Colin, pointed her out: "Mommy, there's my Sunday school teacher." She was a small-framed woman with wispy brown hair haloing her face. And when she sang her face purely glowed.

My husband, four children, and I were newcomers at the church, and ever since we'd joined, Colin had been raving about his teacher. I patted his hand, grateful he liked her, thankful my kids were able to have the kind of Christian experience that had been missing in my own childhood.

While my mother was a traditional Christian, my father was not. They were divorced, and I'd lived with my mother, brother, and sister in a little duplex in California. As the choir sang that Sunday morning, I recalled those days vividly, especially the year I was eight. That was when Mama got cancer. We had a picture of Jesus on our living room wall, and sometimes Mama would look at it and say that if she died Jesus would take her to heaven, where she would watch over us.

One night I awoke to find Mama bending over the double bed where all of us children were sleeping. I watched dream-like as she kissed each of us. The next morning she was gone. She'd been taken to the hospital, where she died that same day. She was forty years old. I thought about what Mama had said, that she would go to heaven and watch over us. More than anything, I wanted assurance that it was true.

I went to live with my father. He didn't believe Mama was in heaven. He explained that her soul had gone to sleep. Period. With time and tutoring I came to believe as he did, that death was an ending, that there was no consciousness, just the mist of eternal slumber.

That's pretty much the idea I'd lived with all my life. Then a few years ago I found a deeper, personal relationship with Jesus Christ. Now I was trying to believe in God's beautiful promise of eternal life. But to be honest, it was difficult sometimes to put those deeply ingrained doubts behind me.

After the service at church that Sunday morning, I made a point to meet Colin's teacher. Gloria Marshall was a single parent with three children; she worked at a center for mentally handicapped children. As we talked, I had the compelling feeling that she was someone I should get to know better.

In the weeks to come, however, I saw her only occasionally at church functions. Then one December afternoon I plopped into a dining room chair to read the church newsletter. Inside was a note from Gloria thanking the church for supporting her as she faced a recurrence of her cancer. *Cancer?* Why, I didn't even know she was sick!

As I sat there, Tiger, our old tabby, slinked over and purred against my leg. I rubbed the cat's ear, a sudden idea nibbling in my thoughts. In my work as a stress counselor I often used positive mental imagery to help clients find healing. Maybe Gloria would consider working with me, no charge.

She was more than willing, and we began therapy sessions in January, meeting weekly in my office and at home. Gloria and I experimented with various meditations and visualizations that would help her envision God's love and healing being released into her life. Inviting a healing image into the mind can have a powerful effect on the body, and Gloria and I kept searching for the one just right for her.

One day as we began our session, a unique, imaginative image popped into my head. "Close your eyes, Gloria," I told her. "Call up a picture of a winged horse." As she followed my direction, I said, "Imagine that he has been sent to you by God and he can fly you anywhere you choose to go. Now climb upon his back and let him take you to your own special healing place."

Maybe it was whimsical, but after a few minutes, when Gloria opened her eyes she was more relaxed than I'd ever seen her. "Oh, Nikki," she cried. "He took me to the most beautiful garden, where I walked and talked with Christ. There were flowers and springs of water."

The winged-horse meditation became her favorite. Again and again she would travel to the imaginative garden to meet the reality of Christ's presence. During her communion she often pictured Jesus giving her "living water" from the springs along the garden paths.

As spring came and went, a bond of closeness formed

between us. Best of all, Gloria improved. An exam showed her inoperable tumor was actually shrinking. "Whatever you're doing, keep doing it," her doctor said. And we did.

Meanwhile, Colin's attachment to Gloria deepened too. She became his most beloved babysitter. One weekend Gloria kept Colin so that my husband and I could get away for some time together. When we returned, Colin was quieter than usual. That night I tucked him in bed, planting a kiss on his forehead.

"Mommy, what will happen to Gloria if she dies?" he asked.

"Gloria will live in heaven with Jesus," I answered, hoping he did not sense the uncertainty in my voice.

Colin closed his eyes, but the little frown of worry remained on his face.

Gloria had been progressing for six months when the change began. Gradually I noticed her energy waning. She grew thinner. Soon the doctor confirmed my fear: the tumor was growing again.

Before long Gloria was unable to go on with our sessions. At our last one she presented me with a ceramic figure she'd made herself, a pastel blue horse. A winged horse.

"I will not give up hope, but I have to face the possibility I may die," she told me. "Perhaps the healing garden in my meditation is really heaven." She said it with such peaceful simplicity that I thought my heart would break.

"No—" I protested.

Gloria knew I struggled with doubts about the hereafter, and she interrupted me, a twinkling light in her eyes. "When I die, I'm going to be your best guardian angel, Nikki. I'll still be around; you'll see."

Autumn arrived. I threw myself into a busy schedule. I called Gloria often. Her voice seemed weak, like a sound fading in my ear. But while the leaves turned loose and drifted away, Gloria held on.

It was during the Christmas Eve service at church that I

discovered her condition had suddenly worsened. After church I hurried to her house. Gloria's bed was surrounded with people speaking in hushed tones. "She's in a coma," her mother told me.

I lifted Gloria's hand into mine. "It's Nikki," I said. "I'm here. I love you." Her eyelids flickered. For a moment she seemed on the verge of speaking, then she lapsed back into her comatose sleep. I squeezed her hand and left. Outside, Christmas tree lights flickered in windows along the street. I knew I would not see Gloria again.

At home I retreated into my office, feeling desolate. Oddly, the pain of losing Gloria kept mingling with memories of my mother. I remembered that my mother had died at the same age Gloria was now, of the very same disease.

Oh, Gloria . . . I picked up the ceramic winged horse from my desk, thinking of the garden she had visited in her meditations. If only there could be a place like that!

Gloria died early Christmas morning. During the late afternoon, we attended her memorial service at the church. Gloria had requested we sing the French carol "Angels We Have Heard on High." But even when we sang the chorus, "Gloria in excelsis Deo," setting Gloria's name to angelic music, I could find little peace.

Later I stood before my bedroom window. The night was cold and starry. I gazed into the darkness for a long while, then went to bed, exhausted.

In the wee hours of the morning I awoke from a deep sleep, strangely alert. I cannot begin to explain what happened next. I simply felt what I thought to be the cat sink onto the foot of the bed against my feet. Tiger knew good and well she was not allowed on the bed. I moved my foot to nudge her to the floor, but she was not there. Then I remembered . . . I had put Tiger outside for the night.

I peered through the shadows. There was nothing on my bed at all, but the weight remained! It pressed against my feet, unmistakeably, gently.

Suddenly a peculiar warmth glowed in the room as if it were enveloped by an electric blanket. My friend Gloria was there. I knew it. The certainty of it seemed indisputable to me.

I do not know how long I lay there with the mysterious pressure on the foot of my bed, but I had the overwhelming feeling that any moment I might actually see her sitting there.

Gradually, though, the weight on the bed disappeared. As it did, my mind was seized by a mental picture, like a movie playing on a screen inside my head. I saw Gloria in white, walking through a garden of unspeakable beauty, a garden blooming with bright flowers and flowing with streams of silver water. I saw her reach out her hand to a shining figure who I knew was Christ.

The image faded. I drifted into tranquil sleep.

When the alarm buzzed some hours later, the room was harsh with sunlight. I climbed from the bed, trying to come to grips with the experience of the night before. In the cold light of day, my intellect wanted a rational explanation. How could such a thing have happened? Was it some imagined illusion? Or had Gloria actually reached across the gulf to give me the assurance I needed so desperately in my life?

Bewildered, I wandered into the hallway. There I bumped into Colin, hurrying from his bedroom. His face was lit with wonder, with that special look a child gets when he sees something wonderful for the very first time.

"Mommy," he said, "why was Gloria sitting on my bed last night smiling at me?"

I gazed into his small upturned face, transfixed. Precisely at that moment I remembered Gloria's words: "When I die, I am going to be your best guardian angel. I'll still be around; you'll see."

I took Colin in my arms. "Perhaps Gloria came to assure you she is fine," I said full of certainty.

Today, two years after Gloria died, I still marvel at the

glimpse of another reality which God granted to Colin and me that Christmas. I don't know why it happened. I only know I found the assurance I had longed for all my life—that death is merely a portal into another dimension, a heavenly dimension, which like the garden in Gloria's meditation brims with beauty and life and the radiant presence of Christ.

IN MOTHER'S ARMS
Eleanor Sass

*W*hen my mother died in 1983 I didn't feel depressed. Mother had lived a long and fulfilled life. Now she was with the Lord, so I felt peaceful about that. Still, I missed her a lot and she was often in my thoughts.

Every now and then I'd dream of my father, or another deceased relative. But I never dreamed about my mother. Sometimes I wondered why. After all, I'd loved her dearly. She'd loved me. And, as far as I knew anyway, I wasn't harboring any deep-down resentments.

Years passed. Then my beloved eighteen-year-old dachshund, Heidi, died. As an unmarried woman living alone, I had no immediate family. Heidi had been my family. We'd spent a lot of time together, going for long walks, or visiting friends in the country on weekends. I'd even taken her with me on a number of my vacation trips.

The night after Heidi died I had a dream. In the dream I could see her. She was being held by someone. It was my mother.

THE LIFTED CURTAIN
Edward K. Leaton

Certain I am that God from time to time chooses to reveal Himself to us. Sometimes He comes to us in moments of stark drama, sometimes so softly, so unobtrusively, that only our souls seem to have seen Him . . .

For many years my wife and I waged a life-and-death battle for our two sons, both of whom had muscular dystrophy. Only when the long, long struggle was over did we realize that God had revealed Himself to us. Yet we would have missed His visit had it not been for a good friend, Edwin Ferree—and for our church.

Ed and Henrietta Ferree, and my family belong to St. Paul's in Darien, Connecticut, and when I say "belong," I mean just that. It is part of us and we are part of it, part of the Body of Christ on earth, and, as the Bible says, "we bear one another's burdens." This is not just a pretty phrase; it is something that became a living daily reality as we watched the day-by-day, year-by-year deterioration of our two growing boys.

My son Ken was three years old when doctors diagnosed his slowness in walking as muscular dystrophy, Duchenne-type. Prognosis was for progressive deterioration of his muscles until, sometime in his teens, those muscles necessary to life itself would be affected.

A few weeks after we received this verdict, Ken's younger brother, Billy, was born, suffering from the same condition.

Several years later, Jan and I, knowing we would have Ken and Billy so short a time, determined to enjoy every day together to the utmost. And there was much to enjoy as the boys walked and talked and explored their world. But with this disease every gain is temporary. Ken, being older, was the first to move into a wheelchair. Some days I would come home to find Jan shut in an upstairs bedroom, tears streaming down her face, while downstairs the therapist painfully straightened bent legs and uncurled clenched fingers.

The strain on Jan as they grew older was enormous: toileting the two large boys, dressing them, feeding them. As Ken's circulation slowed he had to be turned in bed throughout the night. One morning I came downstairs to find Jan, head down, asleep at the dining room table; she'd been catching naps between trips to the downstairs room where the boys slept.

At last in June, 1968, when Ken was fourteen, Billy, eleven, we entered them both in New Britain Memorial, a hospital specializing in long-term and terminal cases. We could probably have managed Billy at home for another year, but it seemed to us that hospitalization would be traumatic enough without separating the boys as well. Billy, with his mop of straight black hair and huge hazel eyes, had never had the muscle control of lips and tongue to speak clearly. Only Ken seemed to have no trouble understanding him. They would talk by the hour, Ken's blond head bent close to Billy's dark one, the older boy interpreting the younger one's thoughts for the rest of us. We knew they must stay together.

To Jan and me the move to the hospital was defeat, the

moment we'd been dreading for so many years. But for Ken and Billy, surprisingly, it turned out to be an exhilarating change. Here, instead of being the ones who forever needed help, they discovered that they had help to give.

In the young people's wing at New Britain everyone who possibly could attended the regular public high school in town, in wheelchairs, even on stretchers, their life-support machinery going with them via the ramps and wide doorways the townspeople had provided. Ken soon found himself helping kids all over the ward with their schoolwork.

Billy, who could still maneuver his own wheelchair, found delight in push-wheeling other young patients into the rec room or to the bedsides of friends.

Having turned our precious sons over to the care of others, and finding that their world did not collapse, Jan and I began to wonder whether in other ways we were relying too much on ourselves alone. It was at this point in our lives that we began the great experiment at St. Paul's, turning ourselves, our family, every detail of living over to the Lordship of Jesus.

It was the beginning of a whole new way of perceiving reality. Not us and our problems in a box over here, others in their separate boxes over there, but all of us at St. Paul's sharing our heartaches, our defeats and victories, together. And one of the parishioners whom we drew especially close to was Edwin Ferree. When Jan and I didn't understand some spiritual concept, when something was too hard for us, we could use Ed's understanding, Ed's strength. It was that real and simple.

Nearly four years after the boys entered New Britain, Billy caught pneumonia. The doctors saved him, but he could no longer breathe without machinery. He was moved to the Intensive Care Unit on the floor below, where his older brother could be wheeled to visit him each day.

For four months, while Ed Ferree and the others at St. Paul's supported us in prayer, Jan and I made the hundred-thirty-mile round trip to New Britain almost every evening. Our invariable routine was to visit Billy first, then go up and be with Ken.

On August 30, 1972, however, for no reason we could have explained, we went first to Ken. He was full of the visit he'd had with Billy. "They let me stay twice as long as usual because Billy's feeling so good. He wasn't even stuttering much."

Down in Intensive Care we found Billy just as Ken had said, hazel eyes shining as he watched television through the tubes and wires linking him to his life-support system. The TV was tuned to the Munich Olympics: With obvious delight he was watching the Russian gymnast, Olga Korbut. Like many handicapped youngsters Billy was fascinated by physical perfection. Olga was his heroine.

Her flawless routine ended, he turned to us. "I'm going to do all those things!" he said, pronouncing each word distinctly. "Just like she did."

It wasn't a question or a wish, it was a statement of fact.

"Billy!" cried Jan, leaning over him. "What's the matter?" His color, so ruddy a moment ago had turned a sickly blue.

In an instant a nurse was at the bedside, then the doctor. But in spite of all they could do, Billy slipped gradually into a deep coma.

Through the long evening I kept thinking about the tenderness of God. If Ken had died first as in the normal course of the disease he would, being three years older, stammering Billy would have been left without his link to his world. And so in spite of all medical probability the Lord was taking the younger boy first.

Peggy, the night-duty nurse came on. The clock crept to midnight . . . 1:00 A.M. . . . 2:00 A.M. And at that moment Billy's eyelids fluttered open. His hazel eyes found Jan.

"Thank you, Mom."

Then me: "Thank you, Dad."

Then they opened wider still, looking not at us, but beyond, at something we could not see. "Oh!" he cried out. Then with a joyous shout: "God!"

His eyelids closed; he was again in deep, unreachable coma. Peggy and I bent over the bed; Jan closed her eyes, praying. After about twenty minutes something like a warm breeze blew past me in the still air. The same instant Jan opened her eyes.

"Billy's gone," she said.

"I know."

At three o'clock we went upstairs and woke Ken. He made us tell over and over again about the look on Billy's face as the curtain between earth and Heaven drew aside. When the day nurse came on Ken asked her, "Can I be the one to tell the kids about Billy? I want to tell them he wasn't afraid and I'm not going to be, either."

Before leaving the hospital we telephoned Ed Ferree who had given us so much support. How glorious to tell him that we *knew* Billy was with Jesus.

I kept wondering if Billy were already swinging from the high bars in some heavenly arena. Back flips, somersaults, handstands . . . just like Olga.

And then a year and a half later, we were driving home from New Britain one final time. Nineteen months had passed since Billy's death. Time for Ken to graduate from New Britain High, to cast his vote by absentee ballot, to handle his lonesomeness by befriending new youngsters entering Memorial, especially those with speech defects: "I can understand him, nurse. You see, he talks a lot like my little brother did."

That afternoon, March 23, 1974, Ken had died. Only— this time—Jan and I had not been there. We had arrived at the hospital around 3:30 on a perfectly routine visit, to be told that Ken had passed away very unexpectedly an hour before.

Why? I wondered, all the long drive home. Why couldn't we have got there one little hour sooner? I turned off the parkway at our home exit. I'd been so sure that the Lord would give us some new reassurance, some fresh glimpse of His Presence, when Ken had to leave us, too.

I pulled into our driveway. What were we going to tell the people at church, this time? I'd phone Ed Ferree; he'd help us think of what to say. Inside the house I dialed the number as slowly as I could. This would be as big a shock to Ed as to us.

"Ed Ferree speaking." There was his voice on the line.

"We're just back from New Brit . . ."

"Ken's with Jesus," said Ed.

It was a moment before I could find my voice. "Yes, Ed. But how could you . . . ?"

It happened at 2:30, said Ed. He hadn't been thinking about Ken especially, in fact he was down in his study digging some papers out of a drawer, when all of a sudden it was as though a movie were unrolling on a screen in front of his eyes. There before him was Ken, tall and straight, striding like a long-distance hiker up a grassy hillside, his blond hair glowing like gold in the bright air.

Then, as Ed watched, Ken came to a swift-flowing stream and stopped, apparently uncertain how to get across. At that moment Ed saw coming down the hill a shining figure that he knew to be Jesus. The radiant Being came to the edge of the stream and stretched His hand across to Ken. Ken reached out, clasped it, stepped easily across. The next moment both had turned and were climbing the hill together, hand in hand.

"That's what you called to tell me, wasn't it?" said Ed. "Ken is with Jesus."

The unfinished feeling disappeared. God had lifted the curtain once again. For a moment I had simply forgotten that Jan and I no longer had to depend on our own sight alone, that we had many eyes and hearts with which to know Him.

"Yes, Ed," I said. "That's what I called to say."

God Fashioned a House

Author Unknown

Weep if we may—bend low as ye pray!
What does it mean?

Listen! God fashioned a house. He said:
  "Build it with care."
Then softly laid the soul . . .
  To dwell in there.

And always he watched it—guarded it so,
  Both day and night:
The wee soul grew as your lilies do,
  Splendid and white.

It grew, I say, as your lilies grow,
  Tender and tall;
Till God smiled, "Now the house is too low
  For the child, and small."

And gently he shut the shutters one night,
  And closed the door;
"More room and more light to walk upright
  On a Father's floor."

Eight

WHEN
WE
BELIEVE

And Jesus said to him, ". . . All things are possible to him who believes."

—Mark 9:23, RSV

God promises to act in response to our faith. When we commit our lives to Him, believe that He will work and act accordingly, God will do what seems impossible. Sometimes we have to be jolted in order to exercise that faith, as several people whose stories appear here discovered. But when we believe and obey, we can prove the truth of what Alice Lindsay discovered: "I did not make a mistake in obeying God when He asked me to believe Him, trust Him and prove Him."

"Prove Me Now"
Alice A. Lindsay

B ring ye all the tithes into the storehouse, that there may be meat in mine house, and prove me now herewith, saith the Lord of hosts."

Prove God? Put Him to the test? At first the idea seemed utterly presumptuous that a young Oklahoma housewife and mother like me should dare to dare God to prove Himself. Yet that is what Malachi 3:10 was suggesting, and that very verse became the springboard to one of the most profound spiritual experiences of my life.

The year was 1934, one of the terrible Depression years. My husband, Corwin, was fortunate: he had a job. Corwin was an automotive electrician, a mechanic, and he received nine dollars for a week's work; a week being seventy-two hours in six days. We had two children, Betty Ellen and David, and though we felt ourselves fortunate to have food on the table, there was no money, none whatsoever, left over for extras.

Our living conditions were meager, even by 1934 standards. In our little three-room house we used kerosene for cooking and lights, coal for heat, and borrowed a neighbor's telephone in emergencies. Our one luxury was running water and bathroom facilities.

Our lives revolved completely around our church, University Baptist at Sixth and Columbia in Tulsa, not because we had acquired a deeper love for the Lord—that love was always there—but because there was no money for amusements or other social outlets. It bothered me, however, that I could not do more for the church.

From the time that I had accepted Christ as my personal Savior until the Depression hit us hard, I had believed in—and practiced—tithing. This had not been difficult when there was money for the necessities of life with a little left over. But now, when pennies were counted as dollars, we had to stop. I felt that God would understand.

Then something happened. One evening as I was studying my Sunday school lesson I found my entire mind and spirit suddenly come alive as I read that passage in Malachi about tithing that said "and prove me now herewith, saith the Lord of hosts."

God knows that I love Him, I thought. *He knows I am doing all I can to serve Him. He knows that nine dollars a week, thirty-six dollars a month for a family of four is not a living, just a bare existence.* Prove God by reducing that amount by three dollars and sixty cents a month? Would God require that from the small, inadequate amount that I had for my family?

I just couldn't understand why I was so torn apart by that verse of Scripture. I spent a long night searching my soul and praying. How unrealistic it seemed for God to ask me to surrender a part of the very little I had when He could provide so very much for us—indeed He had told us of the abundance He intended for us: "Give and it shall be given unto you; good measure, pressed down, shaken together and running over . . . " (Luke 6:38).

The first thing He did say was "give." Even the widow with her mite had done that—she had given everything—yet I was asked to give but a tenth. In my mind I saw Him taking a small amount and multiplying it, the way He took a few loaves and fed thousands of people. I wondered what He might do with my tithe.

By morning, when that long night was over, I knew that He was not asking me to *test* Him; what He was asking me to do was *trust* Him.

On Saturday, as I did each week, I took my husband's salary of nine dollars and carefully allocated it for the following week's needs. With new determination I put first on my list: tithe, ninety cents. When I came to the end of my absolute needs I was twenty cents short of having enough for the children's milk. Milk was five cents a quart and they must have a quart a day to be properly fed. I went over my list again. Each item had been cut to the minimum. There was only one thing I could do—reduce the tithe by twenty cents. Surely God would understand. I started to change the nine to a seven, but in that instant I felt as though someone had slapped my hand. I could not do it. The words "Prove me! Prove me!" kept burning through my mind. I closed my eyes and said, "All right, God. I will."

The following morning when I dropped God's ninety cents into the offering plate, a wonderful peace came over me. I knew that somehow God was going to take care of everything.

On the following Tuesday morning my last five cents had been spent for milk. My children faced four days without, and yet I found myself going about my work with a joyful anticipation that I could neither describe nor understand.

About eleven o'clock there was a knock on my front door. Answering it, I was confronted by a pleasant, smiling man who introduced himself as Ralph Gibson. He said he had worked with my husband about six years before and had come by to pay back a long overdue loan that he owed Corwin. With that he pressed a bill into my hand and started to leave.

It was a five-dollar bill, and I was so stunned I'm not sure I even said, "Thank you." The only thing I remember clearly was standing on my porch, holding a five-dollar bill in my hand, watching a stranger walk out of my yard as I said, "Thank You, God!

An hour later when my husband came home for lunch, he kissed me and asked the reason for my radiant face.

When I told him, he said: "Honey, there just has to be some mistake. I just barely remember Ralph Gibson, and I'm sure I never lent him money. There just has to be some mistake."

"Ralph Gibson may have made a mistake in thinking he owed you five dollars," I said. "You may be making a mistake in having lent it to him and forgotten it. But the fact that this is a genuine five-dollar bill and I have it in my possession is not a mistake. Neither is it a mistake that the children will have not only milk for the rest of the week, but some badly needed clothing as well. And the most wonderful truth of all is that I did not make a mistake in obeying God when He asked me to believe Him, trust Him and prove Him."

Many times and in many ways since then God has taught me many things through His word, and through the personal touch of His Holy Spirit. But this one lesson will always be, for me, one of the great forward steps in faith. Faith in not only God's goodness, but in His loving, caring providence for all who will dare to trust Him.

MIRACLE ON THE HOMOSASSA
Nelson Hutchinson

*B*ack in those days, our family was very poor. We lived in a small house on the Homosassa River, four miles upstream from the Gulf of Mexico. My father struggled to make ends meet as a commercial fisherman.

To help, my mother and I would gather oysters when they were in season. Other times, we went into the woods and chopped fallen trees into firewood, which we sold to the people in town. On good days, we could make a dollar or two.

This was 1939. It was a bad time. A lot of people were poor. The fortunate people who had jobs earned thirty cents an hour.

That year, my mother joined the Church of Jesus Christ in town. There was no road from our house into town. To get there, we had to go by boat three more miles upstream to the highway and the little village. Even so, my mother was at the church every time the doors opened. She loved the church. It gave her a certain strength that carried her through the ordeal of raising a family in such dark days.

We didn't have a Bible in our home. We couldn't afford one. This was a great sadness for my mother. Week after week, she tried to put a few coins aside, saving for enough to buy a Bible, but time and again some emergency would come up, and she had to use the money for food or clothes or medicine. She never complained, but her face showed her hunger for the word of God in our house.

One day my father came home from work with an empty boat. He had caught nothing. He went into the house discouraged, as though he never wanted to look at the river again.

I watched my mother. She got into the boat, arranged the nets, started the motor and headed downstream. As she later told me many times, she went about a mile toward those vast, shallow flats that reach as far as the eye can see at the mouth of the Homosassa. She cut off the motor. Then she knelt in the bow of the little boat, and she began talking to God.

"Father," she said, "I want a Bible for my home and my children. We don't have any money, and so I need Your help. Let me catch some fish today and I'll take them to the market and buy a Bible before nightfall. I have been working hard, trying to get enough ahead to buy a Bible, but I can't seem to make it. Anything I catch today will be Yours. Please help me."

She started the motor. Standing up, she threw into the water the staff that held one end of the net. Slowly she moved the boat in a circle to close off the net. Even before she had gone halfway, fat mullet began jumping into the net. And by the time she had completed the circle, the trapped area was alive with flouncing fish. My mother had lived on the river over a dozen years, ever since she had married my father at the age of sixteen, and she had never seen anything like this.

As fast as my mother could empty her catch into the boat, the net filled up again. In an hour, there was hardly enough room in the boat for herself and the net. She headed home.

I was on the dock as my mother arrived. The boat was riding so low in the water that I wondered if it had sprung a leak. Then I saw the cargo. I couldn't believe my eyes.

"Come on," Mother called to me. "We're going into town to get our Bible."

We went upstream to the highway, where we borrowed a cart from a farmer, transferred the catch into it, then hurried into town to a wholesaler who sold fish to stores and restaurants. The scales showed that my mother had brought in nearly three hundred pounds of fish. The wholesaler paid three cents a pound for the catch—almost ten dollars, as well as my father could do during a good, seven-day week.

We went directly to a bookstore and bought the best Bible the money could buy. My mother let me carry the Bible as we went back to the river and returned the cart. She let me hold it on my lap as she maneuvered the boat back to our home. That evening, my mother read aloud to us from her own Bible for the very first time.

After nearly forty years, the Bible is still in our family, a bit tattered now from so much use. Every morning, my mother would read the Bible to herself; every evening, she would read aloud to the family. We children studied the Bible as we prepared for our Sunday school classes. And my mother never tired of telling people how she had acquired it.

In December 1976, my parents celebrated their golden wedding anniversary. In the special ceremony at our church, my mother and my father held the family Bible between them—living proof that the miracles of the Bible can come alive today for those who have faith enough to believe in them.

GOD'S DEMANDS

Author Unknown

He never asks me to go anywhere He has not gone,
To face anything He has not faced,
To love anyone He does not love,
Or to give anything He has not given.

HIS TWO STRIPS OF WHEAT

Betty Munson

*W*e had never tithed until that year, that disastrous year.

Before then, if my husband, Cliff, or I had any loose change in our pockets, well, that was our children's

Sunday school offering. We might have given a dollar when the offering plate was passed around. We are farmers, dependent on the unpredictable weather and a lot of other things that can ruin you before you know it. We had to watch out for ourselves first. God got what was left over.

Then one Sunday our pastor began talking about tithing. Not your usual stewardship homily, but a series of sermons— almost like talks, neighbor to neighbor—based on the scriptural injunction to give back to the Lord. Something stirred within Cliff and me during those sermons, as if seeds planted long ago were finally sprouting.

I remembered a novel I'd read when I was in my teens. It was about a man who gave lovingly to his fellowman and encouraged others to do so by his example. I'd been impressed. Not because God gave to him so abundantly in return. No, I was impressed because the point of the story was to show how selfless giving, in and of itself, is pleasing to God.

Not long before we were married, Cliff had read a stirring book about the remarkable industrialist R. G. LeTourneau, a man of faith and great success in business. Cliff was struck by how LeTourneau's commitment to God was so complete that not even his work was separate from his faith. LeTourneau considered God his business partner and was a generous tither.

But we still had plenty of questions about tithing. Because we were dry-land wheat farmers, half our ground was fallowed every summer to conserve the soil moisture in this northern Montana climate. Our income was determined by how well the crop did on the other half of our acreage, and on fluctuating market prices. And of course the strength of the crop itself depended in most part on the weather. Ten percent sounded like an awful lot, especially when we considered how rarely there was anything left over after we got done with all the bills. We just didn't see how we could swing it. Yet it seemed that God always provided for us no matter what we gave in return. We knew we could do more.

We called our pastor over to the house. He explained that we could start small, not the full ten percent. The pledge card, he told us, was not a hard and fast legal agreement with the church but rather a promise to God that we would share with Him the fruits of our labor. The bond was between God and ourselves.

Rather than wait until the crop went to market at fall harvest and then figure up our tithe that way, we decided we'd simply set aside part of our acreage. We called it crop-tithing.

"I reckon two strips ought to be about right," Cliff calculated one day near the beginning of the year. A strip of wheat on our place is a half mile to a mile long—running north to south to protect the topsoil from the prevailing west winds—and maybe eighteen rods wide, a rod being roughly sixteen feet. In a good year we get a yield of twenty bushels or so per acre. We chose a couple of strips on the east end of our producing land. Come fall the yield from these strips would be our tithe. "These two are Yours, Lord," I said.

After we signed our pledge card, Cliff and I felt real good about it. In fact, we began tithing some right away from the little outside work Cliff picked up before harvest season.

But then disaster struck, the kind of thing farmers have nightmares over. An early summer hailstorm cut and pounded our fledgling wheat crop into the ground. Wiped it out. The damage was total. We lost everything. Everything, that is, except those two strips on the east end, the ones we'd crop-tithed. They were unscathed.

Surveying the devastation, I felt the hurt lodge in my throat. I couldn't even cry. I was numb. What would we do now? We had no crop insurance. There would be no income for our family this year. None, unless we used those two remaining strips—two out of thirty!—for ourselves.

"Well," sighed Cliff as we disconsolately kicked through the broken stalks and brown puddles, "we promised those to God."

I nodded. "That still has to be our tithe," I agreed. "There's no going back on it that I can see."

Cliff hooked his arm around my waist. "We'll make do," he said, squinting across our ravaged land. But neither of us could say how.

From that July until next harvest was the toughest financial time we ever had. It wore us down sometimes. But we started to learn to trust in God for every need, every problem. And there were problems.

Cliff went to the bank to borrow operating expenses till the next crop. New management had taken over. Our records had been misplaced. There was no personal relationship to fall back on. Other farmers had to borrow too. The bank lent us the money eventually, but not as much as we thought we needed.

When harvest came that autumn it was a dark period. We cut the two strips, sent the wheat to market and gave the proceeds as our tithe, just as we'd pledged. It made no sense financially, but we couldn't break our bond.

We managed. Cliff went custom cutting that fall, which means hiring out your services to other farms. He had to go farther away than usual, where there were still crops. That winter he worked repairing engines and machinery. Cliff had always been a good mechanic and we'd set him up a nice workshop. The jobs always seemed to come when things looked particularly bleak.

When farmers get in trouble in an area, a lot of other businesses suffer. But our local grocer was still able to help out by letting us charge when we had to. I only bought bare necessities on credit. Christmas that year was looking bleaker and bleaker until Cliff finished a repair job ahead of schedule. We were able to purchase a few inexpensive gifts for the kids.

Naturally I yearned for our usual ample turkey to preside at the center of the holiday table with all the trimmings. This year I couldn't bring myself to charge one. It was not a strict necessity. I didn't even pray for a turkey. I just *yearned*.

Then, on Christmas Eve, a friend showed up at our door with a big turkey as a bonus payment for some work Cliff had done. That turkey was the best-tasting bird we ever had. It was one of our best holidays too, because we felt truly blessed, maybe even more blessed than if we'd had a bumper crop to celebrate.

The Lord was taking care of us.

That winter the soles of our five-year-old's shoes gave out. We prayed. Soon enough Cliff got an extra job that brought in just enough for new shoes. It seemed always to happen that way during the year after our crop was wiped out. We didn't have close to what we were used to, but with prayer and with trust we always managed, and we learned to get by on what was provided.

The greatest blessing of all that year was not material. It was spiritual. God protected us from fear, from worry; for the more we trusted in Him, the more our faith grew that He would watch over us always. Those two tall strips of sturdy wheat that we crop-tithed, *they* sealed that trust.

Malachi the prophet proclaimed, " 'Bring the whole tithe into the storehouse, that there may be food in My house. Test Me in this,' says the Lord, 'and see if I will not throw open the floodgates of heaven and pour out so much blessing that you will not have room enough for it.' "

Ever since that harvest we have tithed a portion of our crops. In good seasons and bad, it is a promise that we keep. It is a promise God returns abundantly, always.

DOUBT
William Blake
(from Auguries of Innocence)

He who doubts from what he sees
Will ne'er believe, do what you please.
If the sun and moon should doubt,
They'd immediately go out.

ADRIFT
Sandy Feathers-Barker

Nothing, it seemed, could spoil that hot, windy day in June. At 10:00 A.M. my husband, Joe, and I pulled out of the driveway of our apartment in Gainesville, Florida, where Joe was getting his master's degree in architecture. Trailing behind our camper-truck was our sixteen-and-a-half-foot sailboat. We were headed for Cedar Key on Florida's Gulf coast.

"Just think, a whole afternoon of sailing," I said. Gringo, our big cinnamon-brown dog, wagged his tail. Joe whistled. It was starting so perfectly.

If anything at all threatened to mar the day it was the problem we'd wrestled with for weeks. Joe would finish graduate school in a couple of months, and after that, life curled up into big question marks: Where should we settle? Which job should we take? I'd worried till I was in knots. But now, as we bounced along the highway, I shoved aside my anxieties about the future. They could wait till I returned.

We arrived at the marina with the sun burning at high noon. As I stepped from the truck, a strong gust of wind squalled through the parking lot. I gazed out at the choppy blue water. A few emerald islands dotted the bay. And beyond that, the Gulf stretched to the horizon, immense and awesome. A peculiar feeling swept through me. Not really foreboding, just uneasiness.

We threw a twelve-ounce bottle of water in the boat, strapped on bright orange life jackets, and slid our sailboat into the water. "Hop on, Gringo," I called. Within minutes the three of us were careening out into the bay. I leaned over the side of our little turquoise boat to steady it against a fresh wind howling from the northeast.

Suddenly we slammed aground on a sandbar. I listened as the sand grated against the boat, hoping the centerboard wouldn't be damaged. Without that slim three-foot stabilizer that serves as a keel, we would lose practically all control.

"I'll shove us off," Joe yelled, pushing with an oar. Suddenly we broke free. Joe struggled to tack to the deeper channel waters. But something was wrong. The boat side-slipped through the blue-green swells like a car without a driver. The centerboard was obviously damaged. I wondered how badly. We were sliding sideways out of the bay! There was only one last island between us and open sea. The shoreline was shrinking to a green strip in the distance.

"Joe! We're passing the last island!"

"Don't worry, we'll make it," he said. Joe . . . always the optimist.

But around the island, the wind was even wilder. With windswept water slashing over our boat's sides, we were being pitched from wave to wave. I grabbed for terrified

Gringo. "Lord," I whispered, "I think we're going to need Your help." But the gale seemed to tear the words away from my mouth.

Joe seized the anchor and threw it over. "Oh, no!" I screamed as the anchor line tore from its cleat. The rope snaked overboard and disappeared forever.

"Got to get the sails down," Joe shouted over the wind, "or we'll be blown out to sea!" In our haste we did lower them, but we knocked a fitting loose and lost the halyard that we'd need to raise the sail later.

We looked at each other in horrified silence. The only way we could hoist the sail again would be to lower the hinged mast to the deck and re-rig the line from its top. And that required a calm sea and no wind at all.

In desperation, Joe fitted oars into the oarlocks and tried to row. It was hopeless. We reeled on like a toothpick in a torrent. Now the sun was sinking into a fading orange haze. Night was coming . . . darkness on the ocean. I looked back toward land. It was gone. We were lost, blown into the open sea.

Soon darkness surrounded us. Black waves crashed against the boat, showering us with cold water. I shivered in the night wind. Joe helped me wrap up in the sails and we huddled in the cramped, decked-over cockpit area beneath the mast. The boat pitched so violently that we had to lash ourselves down with ropes to keep from going overboard. My body pounded the hard hull of the boat till I ached.

Then seasickness struck. All night as we slid through the dark, twisted labyrinth of water, I lay in agonizing nausea. I wondered . . . was anyone, anywhere, looking for us?

As dawn filtered into a Sunday sky and the relentless wind still blew, I looked out at the most terrifying sight of my life. Water. Everywhere. Like a jagged gray blanket, it stretched on forever.

"Joe, where are we?" I asked.

"We're a long way out," he said grimly. "We were blown southwest."

The sun became a white-hot laser. I licked my parched lips. "We'll have to save our water," Joe said, as he measured out a few sips. I drank, watching Gringo lick the salt water on the boat. How long could we last on twelve ounces of water in this heat?

Hours went by. I craned my neck, searching for an airplane. Not even a sea gull flew this far out. Our boat became a tiny floating island of hopelessness. I remembered the anxieties of yesterday. What to do after Joe finished graduate school suddenly seemed such a small, petty uncertainty.

The waves rolled by like the years of my life. Unconsciously, I laid my hand on Gringo's head. He turned his huge brown eyes up to mine. As I stared down into Gringo's eyes, something profound, yet simple, took place. I saw the look of trust. Trust that, despite everything, I was taking care of him, as always. And like an arrow, a thought came to my mind. *Why shouldn't I trust God just as Gringo was trusting me?*

Across the boat Joe was saying, "We're helpless. If only we could raise the sails again, but it's impossible with the wind and waves this rough."

The thought returned: *Trust.*

I spoke slowly, hesitantly. "Do you remember in the Bible when the disciples were caught in a storm on the Sea of Galilee?"

Joe looked at me strangely. "Go on."

"Jesus calmed the wind and waves for them," I said. "If He did it for the disciples, wouldn't He do it for us?"

So while the sun glowed low and golden on the ocean, we joined hands and prayed. "Please, Lord, we're trusting You to still the wind and water. Amen." Three minutes passed. Four. Five. And then, in a moment so awesome I can still scarcely believe it, the six-foot swells melted into a sheet of still water. The wind stopped abruptly. There wasn't a ripple or a sound.

Frantically we lowered the hinged mast to the deck and retrieved the line for hoisting the mainsail. "It'll work now," Joe said, raising the mast.

Our sails slatted in the still air. "Lord," I said, "we're ready. Please give us wind to blow us back east to shore."

As if the Creator's hand were moving across the sea, a steady wind began to blow. The sun hovered on the water. We were sailing away from it, east toward land! "Praise God," I rasped.

The moon rose in front of us. Since the wind was from the west, we could run before it with no need for our useless centerboard. For twelve hours, Joe clutched the rudder and the line controlling the mainsail. We guessed we'd been blown over a hundred miles out to sea. Yet, if this wind held, we could make land again.

As daylight approached, Joe neared complete exhaustion. We both collapsed in the tiny cockpit to sleep. When we awoke, the sea was a mirror of glass, the world an eerie vacuum of silence. The sails hung limp. What had happened to our east wind?"

"What does it mean?" I asked. Joe shook his head. Gringo paced nervously. Fear mounted in me like a tidal wave. Was this the calm before the storm I'd always heard about?

O God, I thought, You've brought us this far. Why have you left us here?

Trust Me, came the silent assurance. Trust? Stranded, without land in sight, our water gone, our bodies near collapse, and maybe a storm coming. Suddenly, it seemed too much to ask.

Joe crawled into the cockpit in despair. Even he, the eternal optimist, knew. We had reached the end.

I stared at the sea, too desolate to cry. "God," I whispered, "I was counting on You . . . ." I stopped, my breath suspended. For in the distance, coming over the horizon was a cross. I rubbed my eyes and looked again. It was still there. A breathtaking white cross! It seemed to be rising straight out of the water. Was I hallucinating? Seconds later a boat rose beneath the cross. It was a cross-shaped mast. Dear God! It was real! My breath came back in muffled little gasps. A dazzling white boat was plowing right at us.

"Joe," I called, hardly able to find my voice. "A boat!" Joe leaped up, his eyes incredulous. As it churned closer, Joe raised his life jacket to the top of the mast. I waved my arms wildly.

Soon, a fifty-one-foot yacht was before us. Up on deck, an astonished boy peered down at us. "What in the world are you doing way out here?" he called.

I burst into tears as a vacationing doctor and his family appeared on deck and helped us aboard. We gathered around their table below, while the doctor checked his charts. He returned, shaking his head. "The course I set this morning on automatic pilot was eighteen miles off. An eighteen-mile deviation. I can't explain it."

But I could. There in the safe, solid cabin of the doctor's boat, it all ran together. The calming of the ocean, the sudden east wind, then its abrupt ceasing, an eighteen-mile alteration on sophisticated electronic navigation equipment—all this had made their big yacht and our little sailboat intersect exactly in the midst of endless time and water. God—a powerful, ingenious, caring God—had been there through every uncertain hour. And now I knew I could trust Him with every uncertainty . . . including those small, worrisome anxieties about the future still waiting for us at home.

A few hours later a storm smashed into the Gulf, twisting the sea into savage ten-foot waves. But I leaned back, enveloped in the thundering sound of the storm, at peace. My future, like the sea, rested in very good hands.

Not One, But Two
Samuel Hooker

Back when I was pastoring a church in Portland, Oregon, I received a call early one morning from the local hospital. A patient who was dying had asked for a minister of my denomination. Could I come to the hospital as soon as possible?

Half an hour later I was standing at the bedside of Felix Richy as the nurse drew the curtain around us.

"Pastor," Mr. Richy said, "my uncle was a preacher and he used to talk to me about the Lord, but I wouldn't listen. My wife always tried to get me to go to church, but I wouldn't go. Now I'm going to meet my Maker and my life is filled with sin."

"Mr. Richy," I began, "the fact that you admit you've sinned and are willing to confess it is half the battle." We talked. I quoted some Scripture about God's forgiveness, and then we prayed together as he turned his life over to the Lord.

The next day I returned, and the next day and the next, and to the amazement of the hospital staff, Felix kept improving. In a matter of weeks he was sent home, and on the next Sunday he appeared in my church. For eight years he sat in the same pew each Sunday with hardly a miss. In the end he died suddenly of a heart attack.

I officiated at the funeral, and after the burial an elderly man approached me.

"Pastor Hooker," he said, "you don't know me, but I was in the bed next to Felix Richy when you came to the hospital that morning. I wrote down those Scriptures you quoted and gave my heart to Jesus too.

"That morning you didn't catch just one fish, you caught two. I jumped into the net while you were pulling it in."

Nine

WHEN

WE

PRAY

*A*sk and it will be given you. . . . For every one who asks receives.''

—*Matthew 7:7, 8, RSV*

Faith and prayer are inextricably mixed. We express our faith in our prayers as well as in our actions. There are times, though, when we pray with only the tiniest bit of faith. Even then, promised Jesus, ''impossible'' results will come. Because we pray, God meets our needs—for things as big as a baby mattress, as small as a wheel bolt, and as improbable as an invisible rain shield. His answers show us that, as Isaiah put it, ''The arm of the Lord is not too short to save, nor his ear too dull to hear'' (59:1, NIV).

THAT OLD PICKUP TRUCK
Don Bell

B ack that winter of 1950, I wouldn't have said I knew much about praying, but I guess I knew where to turn when I needed help. At the time, Joe Spurgin and I were baching on the Nielson Ranch south of Cody, Wyoming. He was a ranch hand and I was a cowboy, and we were left in charge of feeding and caring for the livestock while the ranch manager, Bill Hill, was away.

When I woke up one February morning it must have been twenty below zero. I know I had to chop ice for the cows' drinking water. I spent most of the day doctoring the animals that were sickly. Then, while Joe stayed back at the bunkhouse, I rode my horse into an area called Oregon Basin to check on the cattle there. Toward evening I headed home, eager for the hot supper Joe would have ready to eat.

I wasn't far from the ranch when I knew something was wrong. No smoke was coming out of the chimney, no sign of Joe. I put up my horse in the barn. Walking away from the stall, I saw blood frozen on the ground. I thought Joe must have butchered a beef. Then in the tack room I saw Joe Spurgin himself, lying on his back with a rifle next to his right arm. I knelt down to check his pulse. It was real weak, but Joe was still alive. *I've got to get him to the hospital,* I thought, *and quick!*

On the ranch we had an old Chevrolet pickup truck. Trouble was, it was hard to start. In the middle of summer we had to push and pull it to get it running, but in the below-zero winter, I could never tell what it would do. I rushed outside, panting in the cold air, and as I ran I said to God, "Please help me start it so I can save Joe Spurgin."

I slid onto the cold leather seat, slammed the door, blew on my hands for warmth, put my foot on the gas pedal and turned the key in the ignition. I couldn't believe my ears. No sputter, no cough! The engine started with one turn of the key.

"Thank You, God," I whispered. "Just keep the engine running." I jumped out, lowered the tailgate and ran back to get my wounded partner.

Now, Joe was a big man, six feet tall and over two hundred pounds. With his long johns, wool shirt, jeans, cowboy boots, overshoes, coveralls and a heavy sheepskin coat, add another twenty-five. How was a man of my size, five feet seven and one hundred forty pounds, going to move this body? "Lord," I prayed, "You helped me get that old pickup started. Now I have another favor to ask. Help me move my friend."

Before I tried to lift Joe's body, I saw he was frozen down in his own blood. I picked up a shovel, slipped it under where the blood had frozen his clothing to the barn's wooden floor and pried him loose. Joe was still unconscious. "Don't die on me," I said, and then somehow I managed to hoist him on my shoulders.

I slipped him into the back of the truck, shut the tailgate and drove wild and fast to the Cody hospital. It was dark by the time I got there.

I backed up to the emergency room door, ran into the hospital, and was met by a doctor I knew well, Dewitt Dominick. I told him in an excited tone of voice that I had a man in my truck who was shot with a .25 caliber Winchester rifle.

Two helpers took a gurney out to the truck and loaded what I feared was a dead man onto it. Then the doctor looked him over and said, "Yep, he's alive. Just barely."

Joe's clothing was cut off him and the doctor found that Joe had been shot in the back of his right knee. The bullet came

out of his ankle. Joe was still pale and unconscious, but I had
to leave him at the hospital and get back to look after the
ranch.

I put in a sleepless night. Next morning I got up early, fed
the cattle, and took care of the ranch chores. I cleaned up,
shaved, grabbed a cup of strong black coffee and went outside
to the pickup. Once again I slid onto the leather seat,
slammed the door, put my foot down on the accelerator, and
turned the key in the ignition.

Nothing. I sat there for a minute, then smiled. *Lord,* I
thought, *You helped me when I needed it most. I can get to the
hospital just fine without this old pickup. You just keep old Joe alive.*

I went out to the road to hitchhike and in a few minutes
caught a ride that took me straight to the hospital. Joe was
sitting up in bed, smiling. He'd had several pints of blood
pumped into him and now a shade of color was back in his
face.

"How'd it happen?" I asked.

"Don, after you rode off yesterday I saw a coyote near the
sheep pen. I ran to the barn and grabbed the rifle that hangs
in the tack room. And that's all I remember. I must have
fainted dead away when I saw all that blood." He shook my
hand and thanked me for saving his life.

Joe got well, but after that he never came back to the ranch
to work. I lost track of him for a while, then heard that he
went to Cañon City, Colorado, where he was employed at
the state prison. He retired after twenty years and moved back
to Billings, Montana, where he had a sister nearby. In 1980
the sister called me and asked if I could come see Joe. He was
dying and had asked for me.

I drove up to Billings and found Joe looking as gray as he
did when I discovered him on the barn floor. Again Joe shook
my hand and thanked me for saving his life. He gave me his
hat, his silver belt-buckle, and all the money he had left in the
world, $150.

"No," I said, "I don't want your money, Joe."

"Take it, partner," he said. "I'm going to die tonight. I'm going to see God, and when I get there I'm going to thank Him for giving me thirty more years to live."

Joe died that night, and all these years I've kept his hat and buckle. They remind me of an old friend and an old Chevy pickup truck, and they remind me that God gives you help just when you need it most.

"Don't Let It Rain Today"
Kennith Bishop

*A*t last, after holding Sunday school in the choir loft and in corners of the sanctuary, the members of our small church finally raised enough money to build an education building.

On the day the concrete floor was to be poured, I woke up at 5:00 A.M. Seeing the sky heavy with clouds, I phoned the contractor to call off the day's work. Rain mixing with the fresh concrete might add an additional expense that our tight budget would not permit. Our dream of a new building might be delayed indefinitely.

By 6:00 A.M., however, with no rain, I made the difficult decision to call and tell the contractor to come after all. But when I arrived at the church to await the workers, rain clouds swirled overhead. I walked to the center of the building site and knelt.

"Don't let it rain today, Lord," I prayed.

Then, thinking about the farmers in this rural community who needed the rain, I changed my request. "Just don't let it rain right here."

Within a few minutes, the crews arrived and prepared the ground for the concrete. The clouds grew more ominous. At noon the workers drove away for lunch. Soon they returned to report that the rains were coming down so hard around them, they couldn't get out of their trucks.

In the afternoon the men worked feverishly, hurrying to finish before the expected downpour. To the east and to the west, rain pounded down.

But that day, on the site where the concrete was poured, the rains never fell.

R A I N
Dawn Adrian Adams

*T*oday was moving day, but as I stared out the window, spattering drops of gray rain turned into a hammering downpour.

It figures, I thought, fighting back the tears. It had been raining on the day my husband left me three months earlier, and as far as I was concerned it had been raining ever since. I was in South Carolina, where we'd moved with our eight-year-old son, Harrison, a year before. I was more than a thousand miles away from my family, barely making ends meet, with bills piling up, fearful of the future without my husband.

At least I'd found a cheaper place for Harrison and me to live. We were moving out of the brick house we'd been renting and into a tiny three-room cottage about fifteen miles away at half the rent. To make the move, I'd borrowed a sorry old pickup truck from work. But I didn't have a tarpaulin to cover our possessions that would go in the back of the truck. So I waited until the rain stopped, then told Harrison to hurry and help me load up.

Onto the truck went a wooden table and chairs, Harrison's bed and mattress, and a studio couch. I piled on cartons and wedged in the lamps.

Just then the wind gusted up. Scanning the dark sky, I wanted to pray. When I was little, Daddy always said, "Make prayer a habit. Then, when there's an emergency and you need it most, praying will come naturally."

Now, though, the words stuck in my throat. I was still going to church, but I felt out of the fold. I'd prayed so hard for my marriage to be saved, but things just got worse, and I found it harder and harder to believe God could do anything.

Now, I thought bitterly, my belongings were about to get soaked. "Dear Lord," I said, "is it never going to stop raining on me?" I shoved the last box into the pickup and slammed the tailgate shut.

As we drove down the highway, the wind grew vicious. Twigs swirled against the windshield and the wind rattled the load stacked high in the back of the truck.

There was a *thunk*. In the rear-view mirror I saw a chair toppling over against a floor lamp. Groaning, I pulled over, put the brake on, and let the engine idle while I stepped out and shoved the chair back in place.

The old truck coughed and stalled. I got back in and turned the key in the ignition. Nothing happened. I swallowed hard and tried again—and again. My fear and exhaustion were too much. I buried my face in my arms on the steering wheel.

I was surprised to feel my son grab my hand and squeeze it the way he'd always done when we'd prayed together. And I heard myself saying over and over, "Please, Lord, help us." I was doing what came naturally—praying. When I sat up I felt more peaceful than I had felt in months.

I turned the ignition key. This time the engine started, and I pulled onto the highway. Ahead of us a dark curtain of rain stretched across the landscape.

"We're driving right into it, Mommy!" Harrison said.

The downpour came nearer and nearer. Now it was only two car-lengths ahead of us. Harrison and I braced for the hammering rain that would hit the truck at any minute.

Only it didn't. Harrison looked all around, then asked, puzzled, "Mommy, why don't we get to where the rain is?"

I was puzzled too. In the side and rear-view mirrors I could see rain beating down alongside and in back of us. There was a curtain of rain on the fields to our right, and as we dipped between two small hills rain pelted a house and barn to our left as well. Every car that passed us had its lights on and sent up sheets of water—but I didn't even have to turn on our windshield wipers.

"Mommy," Harrison said, "it's raining everywhere but where we are!"

"Son," I said quietly, "I think God is going out of His way to let us know that it's stopped raining on *us.*"

That night, after unloading our furniture and packing boxes, I tucked Harrison into bed. A sense of peace filled me. I no longer feared the future. Life's difficulties would not go away. But neither would God's presence and His love.

OUR REFUGE
Nina Willis Walter

Whenever you come to the Lord
   with an earnest prayer,
He is there.

When you come with a contrite heart
   or a human fear,
He will hear.

Though you may have little to give,
   bring Him your best;
He supplies the rest.

THE MIRACLE MATTRESS
John W. Cowart

We kept our newest baby in an egg carton—not one of those Styrofoam ones with pockets for a dozen eggs, naturally, but the large cardboard box that hundreds of eggs come in. My resourceful wife had covered the box with some flannel material printed in nursery scenes, and this makeshift arrangement served well enough as a bassinet. But now the baby was five months old and too big to sleep in the egg carton anymore.

I was struggling through school while working nights,

collecting and counting mosquitoes for the City Health Department in Jacksonville, Florida. If I'd been paid a penny for each mosquito in the traps, instead of by the hour, I could have afforded all sorts of luxuries, such as a crib for our third baby. But supporting a family of five on a part-time job imposes quite a few financial limitations, so the baby slept in the egg carton.

One night in family devotions, my wife explained the whole situation to our Lord. "Dear Jesus," Ginny prayed, "we've just got to have a new crib mattress. Eve is too big for her little box, and she needs a bed. You know we have that old crib in the storeroom, but it was secondhand when we got it. And after Jennifer and Donald outgrew it, that mattress was in tatters, so we need a new mattress. Soon, please. Amen."

Ginny's prayers made me mad. I felt frustrated because I was trying to live as I thought God wanted, and I felt He had let me down. I attended school because I thought He wanted me there. My job seemed to be the place He had for me, and I was trying to raise my family right. But I couldn't even afford a mattress for a secondhand baby crib. It just didn't seem fair.

Another thing complicated our situation. Early in our marriage Ginny and I had decided to attempt to live without buying anything on credit, without ever borrowing money and without ever telling anyone except God about our needs. We have not always stayed within these guidelines, but they represent part of a standard of faith we acknowledge. I suspect the real reason we first aspired to this life-style was that we were too hard-headed, proud, and stubborn to admit how poor we actually were. At any rate, the baby slept in a box, Ginny prayed, and I was mad at God.

One afternoon during the week after Ginny's prayer, one of my fellow students needed a ride to work after school, so I gave him a lift. We had to cross the Main Street Bridge over the St. Johns River. This bridge spans nearly a mile of river and is about a hundred feet above the water. It carries traffic for U.S. Highways 1 and 17 and is one of the most heavily traveled bridges in the city. A huge metal grating in the center of the bridge rises to allow ships to pass underneath in the main channel of the river. As we drove across that metal grating, something lay right in the center of the roadway—it looked like a brand-new crib mattress.

Since a truck was following me closely, I couldn't stop to check. I had to follow the flow of traffic into downtown Jacksonville, where one-way streets forced me to make an eight-block loop before I could head north over the bridge again. All this maneuvering took close to thirty minutes, but when I returned, incredibly, the crib mattress still lay on the grate, untouched by the busy traffic. Right then and there, I stopped being mad at the Lord.

I paused on the center span. My friend leaped out, threw the crib mattress in the backseat, and jumped in the car again as traffic honked behind us. The mattress probably had fallen from the back of a truck or something, and there was no way for me to locate its original owner. Except for a scuffed place at one corner, it appeared to be in perfect condition.

That night as Ginny and I put together our old crib to receive its new mattress, I hesitated. "Suppose it's not the right size for our crib?"

"Hand me the screwdriver," Ginny replied. "God wouldn't send us a mattress that doesn't fit."

She was right.

THE DRIVER
Lynn Erice

There was a storm on its way that December night of 1986, but I didn't know it. Warnings were flashed on TV screens all across the state, but I didn't see them. The radio said not to leave your house unless you absolutely had to, but I didn't hear it. That night I was sitting in my apartment in Rochester, reading, and feeling overwhelmed. I had an impulsive urge to get away and the farm seemed the only place I could go. Feeling lonesome for my mother, I said to Mealie, my dog, "Come on, let's go see Grandma."

Wearing just the clothes I had on, but no hat or boots, I walked out the door with Mealie at my heels. We climbed into my Datsun and headed toward Lyndonville, New York, where I had grown up. I'd left home when I was nineteen. I'd married and lived all over the United States, but always I'd returned. The farm reminded me of the stability I longed for, the security I'd lost.

After a bad marriage, I thought I'd finally made peace with living alone. I had a nice apartment and a steady job waiting tables, but I was lonely and unsure of the future. I'd always thought God had meant me to do more with my life. At thirty-six, I still felt that I hadn't accomplished anything.

The snow was coming down fast as I drove north through Rochester on Interstate 390, heading toward the Lake Ontario State Parkway. That was the most direct route west to Lyndonville, and I could avoid the traffic on the other roads.

There was a problem, though, when I reached the parkway. It hadn't been touched by snowplows and the snow was already inches deep. I turned around at the first exit and drove back to Route 104, a much-traveled, well-maintained highway eight miles south.

"Guess I should have gone this way from the beginning," I told Mealie. "Now we're already twenty miles out of our way."

The snow on 104 looked bad too, but I didn't want to turn back. And I didn't want to admit I was scared. Mealie and I pushed on, driving very slowly, following the red taillights of the car ahead. The wind howled around us and the snow swirled so fiercely that I could see nothing else but those red taillights. It seemed pointless to turn back. After all, the weather would be just as bad going east as it was going west and I wouldn't have any taillights to follow. In two hours of driving, not a vehicle had passed me going in the opposite direction.

Suddenly the red taillights stopped. A man stepped out and fought against the wind. As I rolled down my window to talk to him, the wind gushed in so hard that I could barely breathe.

He leaned down to me. "I'm stopping," he said. "I can't see anything at all now."

"Where are we?"

"Somewhere near Albion."

Albion! I had been driving two hours and was only as far as Albion! That's usually only a thirty-five-minute trip.

Trying to sound calm, I said, "I guess I'll keep going. There's no sense for me to stop here. I'm only going to Lyndonville."

"Okay," he said. "Good luck."

Within moments of leaving him, I had second thoughts. It was obvious that we had been the only two cars on the road. Now I was alone. Maybe I should go back, but why? I only had fifteen more miles to go.

I drove on. I was traveling alone in a vast expanse of whiteness, a sort of no-man's-land. The only way I stayed on course was by making out the mailboxes along the road. Now and again I veered toward one, and shaking with fear, I'd have to stop and maneuver my way onto the road again. Sometimes a glimpse of light beckoned from a faraway house. I was tempted to stop and try to make it on foot to the light. But wearing only jeans, a sweater and sneakers, I was not prepared for a difficult walk through a blizzard. And if I stopped the car and stayed in it, the snow was coming down so fast that we would soon be buried under it.

Minute by minute, second by second, my mind raced along. My hands ached, locked around the steering wheel in a vicelike grip of fear and concentration. My body was so tense that it felt as though it were ready to break into pieces.

Now most of the windshield was covered with ice. The buildup on the wiper blades was so great that their rubber surfaces couldn't even make contact with the glass. Visibility was so poor that everything looked the same—a surreal landscape of stark white.

I could only inch forward. Suddenly the car jolted to a stop and in the split second it took for me to realize that I'd plowed into a snowbank, I screamed. Frantic, wild with fear, I began to argue with myself. "You fool, now you've done it. You'll never get out."

Calmly, something inside me said, *Just back out slowly. Drive out the way you came in.*

"No, you're stuck. You'll stay there and freeze to death. Mom won't even find out for days. Poor Mealie. She's afraid."

Back out slowly. It can be done.

Finally I took my mind's advice. Trying to calm Mealie in the seat beside me, I backed out slowly. My body sagged with relief. I straightened the car out and we started moving forward again. But what was the use? I peered desperately out the windshield. There was nothing but snow. No road, no lights, no mailboxes, just snow.

Shaking my head in disbelief, my eyes flooding with tears, I cried out, "Lord, help me. Please, Lord, I can't drive anymore. I can't go on. Take over. Please, Lord, drive this car for me."

No sooner were those words out of my mouth than something wondrous began to happen. Ahead, where moments before all had been white, a tiny spot of clear highway shone in my headlights. I drove toward it and then there was another little clearing in the road. And then another and another. To my astonishment we kept moving forward, foot by foot, yard by yard.

"Thank You, Jesus," I prayed. In my desperation I had called out to Him and He answered. He was with me in the blizzard. Wouldn't He be with me always?

I drove on—or should I say the Lord drove. I sat in the driver's seat with my hands on the wheel, but I knew I wasn't driving. Gradually my courage returned and my tears disappeared. He was showing me I wasn't alone. I never had been.

Suddenly a set of tire tracks appeared from nowhere. I followed them until I was only three miles from the farm. At that point, after almost three and a half hours of driving, I finally saw a snowplow coming toward me in the opposite direction. Passing it, I switched lanes, taking advantage of the road it had cleared.

When at last I made it to the farm, Mealie jumped out of the car, and we both hurried into the warmth of the house. But now I felt secure. Like the psalmist, I knew for a fact that the Lord is my shepherd. He had brought me home.

THE BOLT IN THE ASPHALT
Stephanie Burt

*L*ast summer I went with my church youth group on a mission trip to the Bahamas, where twice a day we performed a puppet show for youngsters in parks and schools. And twice a day, it seemed, our old school bus broke down.

One hot afternoon we were on our way to a performance when the bus came to a sudden halt. "Not again," everyone grumbled. Our youth leaders, Bill and Daryl, stepped out to see what was wrong.

Up until then I had maintained a good attitude about the bus's unreliability, but this was the last straw. We were stuck on a deserted side street in the sweltering heat with not even a phone booth nearby to call someone for help.

"Guys," Daryl reported, "this is serious. Our clutch has broken and the bolt that holds it together has fallen off somewhere back on the road. We had a big bucket of spare nuts and bolts, but not one of them fits. Just pray."

We joined hands and fervently asked God for help. When we looked up, we saw an odd sight. Bill was kneeling on the pavement, picking something out of the asphalt with his pocketknife. He leaned under the hood of the bus with the object, then came to us with a big smile on his face.

"As you were praying, I looked down and there beside the tire, embedded in the pavement, was an old bolt. On an outside chance I dug it up and screwed it on. It fit!"

The bus started up again and we drove to the puppet show, filled with awe at the power of prayer.

Ten

WHEN

WE

SEE

CHRIST

*T*he Lord said to him in a vision, "Ananias."
And he said, "Here I am, Lord."

—*Acts 9:10,* RSV

Jesus promised us that He would always be with us, and that he would send us a Comforter, just like Himself, to be with us forever. So even though we do not see Jesus with our physical eyes, or in a vision, we trust Him and His promise. Occasionally, however, the curtain is drawn back, and Jesus Christ shows Himself to individuals. For some whose stories are included here, Jesus appeared to them in their desperate situations, to assure them they would ultimately be all right. To others, Jesus revealed Himself in "ordinary" circumstances.

Though we ourselves may not receive a vision of Christ, all the stories in this volume call us to trust Him, to give our lives to Him, and to live in His presence.

THE INCREDIBLE RESCUE
Robert Bowden

I'm a carpenter, an ordinary man who works hard with his hands. I say this because the experience I'm going to tell you about is a strange one, and I want you to know I'm not the kind of man to go around making up outlandish stories.

The winter of 1971 was a tough one for the building trades in Monmouth County, New Jersey, where my family lived. I write country-western music on the side and play the guitar and sing, so I was able to pick up a few jobs on weekends, but not enough to support my wife and three kids.

Then, just before Christmas, I landed my first solid job in months, on the nuclear power plant that was under construction at Salem, New Jersey, 129 miles from our home in Oakhurst. I was grateful for the work, even though it meant I had to live at a motel in Salem and got home to see my family only on weekends.

The nuclear plant was a massive project, involving over four thousand men. I was on the crew building the huge 250-foot cooling towers, like the ones at Three Mile Island in Pennsylvania. My particular job was to erect the wood platforms and the wooden forms—plywood sheets nailed to heavy frames—into which the concrete for the thick tower walls was poured.

All my working life I was used to heights, but climbing the steel to the tops of those towers, as high as a twenty-story building, made me nervous. On such a vast project there often are lots of injuries. Every day we heard stories of men losing fingers and toes, and even arms and legs.

One clear, sunny day in February, it was bitterly cold. I was glad I'd be working inside the tower, fairly close to the bottom, out of the wind, stripping the forms off the hardened walls.

Before I had been at the site ten minutes, the cold was numbing my fingers. High above, sunlight streamed through the circular mouth of the tower. Around me, in the freezing semi-twilight at the bottom, there was bedlam as the workers swarmed over the scaffolding. From the unfinished floors, a bristling bed of upright steel construction rods protruded.

I grabbed a hammer and a stripping crowbar and paused, looking up at the platform where I'd be working thirty-five feet above the floor.

"Hey, Jake!" I called to the foreman, my breath steaming the frigid air. "You only got one plank on that platform!"

"It's all right, Bob," he said, trotting over. "If we put up another plank, you won't have room to pull the forms away from the wall. Just be careful."

"Okay," I replied, but I was doubtful. An eight-inch-wide board isn't much to stand on.

I climbed up and began prying the forms loose. It was slow and hard, working so close to the wall on that shaky plank, and the plywood forms were heavy and awkward to handle.

By ten o'clock I had managed to get one off. I paused to warm my numbed hands. Down below, I could see my co-workers picking their way through the forest of upright steel rods. Nasty things. They were for reinforcing the floor; each one was five-eighths of an inch thick, and they varied in height from one to three feet. Their tips were flat. All the same, I had seen a fellow worker impaled on such rods about two years before. All it took was one careless move . . .

I began prying the second form loose. It wouldn't budge; it was stuck to the concrete. I pulled harder. Suddenly the crowbar slipped, throwing me off balance. I plunged forward toward the foot-wide opening where the other plank ordinarily would have been. I knew I was falling. Fear tore through me. I cried out, "God, help me!"

Then, incredibly, it happened. The wooden form and the gray wall of the tower vanished in a blaze of brilliant white light. In the middle of that beautiful, clear light, yet not part of it, stood a Man. He was dressed in a white robe made of some kind of silky cloth. There was a rope around His waist and sandals on His feet. His head was covered by a hood that appeared to be part of the robe. Framing the Man's face, and just visible under the hood, was dark brown, shoulder-length hair. He had a beard with a small part in the middle. His dark brown eyes were commanding but kindly.

Then He spoke. The voice was not in my head, but a real, external voice, beautiful and deep, and it seemed to echo. There is a verse in the Bible that reminds me of it: "And his voice was like the sound of many waters" (Revelation 1:15, RSV).

As long as I live, I will never forget His words: "Son, I am going to save you. Just trust in Me. Don't fight Me."

Then He vanished. And I was falling, plunging face down toward those upright steel rods, each one a dagger.

Strangely, all fear had left me. As my body hurtled down toward death, I thought: *Should I try to save myself somehow? Is there anything I can grab . . . ?* There was nothing.

Don't fight Me, the Man's voice echoed through my mind. I abandoned myself to whatever might happen.

Suddenly, I felt some kind of Power turn my body. Now I was no longer falling face down but sideways, rigidly, like a ruler on edge.

I slammed down between the steel rods. My back grazed the concrete floor, then I was jerked up as if on a giant string, bouncing crazily. Then everything was still.

Everybody came running. "Oh, my God! My God!" Jake kept saying.

"He landed on the rods—they're clean through him!" someone cried.

"I can't look! I'm gonna be sick!" somebody else said.

"No . . . no . . . I'm all right," I gasped. "Cut . . . my belt . . ."

A couple of guys rushed in to cut my belt. Suddenly I could breathe again.

"Good God!" Jake said. "I've never seen anything like this. How come those rods didn't go through him?"

My plummeting body had passed between the rods. The belt loop on my pants had snagged the tip of the tallest rod, about three feet above the floor. Miraculously, the loop held, breaking the force of my fall. Except for grazing my lower back on the concrete, I was suspended above the other rods.

Gently my co-workers lifted me off the rods and laid me on the floor. They gasped in shocked surprise when, a few seconds later, I stood up.

"I don't believe it!" one of the guys said. "He should be dead, but he's standing here!"

"Bob, the Lord was with you today," Jake said, "or this never could have happened."

"That's right, Jake," I said fervently, "the One who saved me was Jesus Christ. He gets the credit!" I was about to tell them what I had seen, but something stopped me. I figured they'd never believe me, in spite of the miracle they had just witnessed.

At the hospital, X rays revealed no broken bones. My only injury was a large bruise in my lower back, where it had hit the floor. The doctor prescribed muscle relaxants and sent me home.

The next morning, my co-worker John, who also lived at the motel, was surprised to see me at breakfast.

"You're not going in today, old buddy, are you?" he asked.

"Sure," I replied, munching a piece of toast. "I'm okay."

"God was really with you yesterday, Bob," he said, studying me.

I looked back at him, and decided to tell him the truth. "John, just as I fell off that scaffold I saw Jesus Christ."

He slowly lowered his cup and looked away. "That's impossible."

"No," I replied firmly, "it's not impossible. I saw Him, and He saved my life." Then I told him about the vision.

"Bob," he said after I had finished, "it's not that I doubt your word . . . but I still think it's impossible. Still, you're here today, alive and healthy . . . so maybe it's not so impossible."

All that day I found myself wondering why the Lord had shown Himself to me and had saved me. Why had I been singled out for a miracle? Did the Lord want me to do some great work in the world? How could I? I was just an ordinary workingman . . .

All of this happened quite a few years ago. I'm still a carpenter, and I still write songs and play and sing. If God has a big job for me, it's still in the future, but I'm open to it. Meanwhile, I just try to be helpful and kind to troubled people wherever I meet them. That's something I can do right now—it's something we all can do.

Sometimes, when I think people will accept it, I tell them about the day when I saw Jesus and He saved my life. And their eyes light up with hope. They know that even if they can't see Him, if He reached down and helped Bob Bowden out of a tight spot, then He'll surely help them, too. And I'm reminded of the words of Jesus Himself: "Because thou hast seen me, thou hast believed: blessed are they that have not seen, and yet have believed" (John 20:29).

WHAT'S THE DOCTOR'S NAME?

Sam Nix

*H*ere in South Korea, where I'm stationed with the U.S. military, I recently met Ms. Kyong Cha Lee, a woman who had suffered a terrible loss.

Ms. Lee's house, like many older homes in Korea, is heated by large charcoal briquettes placed under the floor. During a cold spell last spring this primitive heating system malfunctioned, spreading poisonous carbon monoxide fumes throughout the house, almost killing Ms. Lee.

She lay in the hospital in a coma for days, with her family at her bedside. When she finally awoke, they were too grieved to tell her the extent of her loss. But she astonished them when she said she already knew her two children had been killed in the tragedy. "The doctor told me when he came to look after me," she explained.

"What doctor?" they asked.

"The doctor who prayed by my side and promised that God would watch over me."

They assured her they had seen no such visitor and they had been with her constantly. The physician must have been a dream, they said.

When Ms. Lee was well enough to go home, she was making her way out of the hospital when she caught sight of a portrait in the lobby. "There," she said, "that's the doctor who came to my bedside. What is his name?" "Jesus Christ," came the answer.

And that's the story I heard from Ms. Lee at a retreat recently. She was there with a number of others who, like her, were new in the Christian faith.

THE LONER
Susan Peoples

The shadows in the canyon were already deepening to purple by the time my friend David and I left the biting cold of the mountain river to climb back up the ridge to the mesa above, where we'd stashed our heavy hiking gear. Wearing only tee shirts and jeans, we had earlier descended a gentler slope to one side, drawn by the sight of that idyllic valley so far below. Now, looking up from the dusky canyon floor toward the looming cliff face, still rimmed at the top in gold from the rays of the setting sun, we decided to avoid the easier path and to climb straight up into the light.

The challenge suited me. I was proud of my strong, lean body—proud of my "toughness," my independence.

As we started the climb, I glanced toward David, whom I had met just a couple of weeks before. I had to admire his own lean strength as he nimbly scaled that rocky wall. I felt I could like him very much if I would choose to do so, but I'd fought against the idea—was still fighting it. Any kind of closeness to another human being seemed to me to be a dangerous thing. To invite a person to come near meant also to invite emotional pain, and *that* I could do without. I'd watched my parents suffer through a divorce when I'd been a child, and I hadn't liked what the stress did to them, or to me. I'd decided to keep everyone at a distance, surround myself by an invisible wall. I would shut out all emotion and become totally self-sufficient.

I'd succeeded in that goal. After growing up and leaving

home, I'd held several different jobs, one of them as manager of a restaurant. That, too, had been a challenge, but I'd liked being in charge of a business. Just as I liked being in charge of my own life and destiny, climbing up this cliff.

As the way grew steeper, edging toward vertical, I constantly tested the stability of the rocks before trusting them with my weight. Several times I found a rock to be loose and I searched for a different handhold or foothold before moving higher. Soon I had ascended almost two hundred feet. I glanced again toward David, seeing that he was off to one side and a little higher than I. We had only thirty or so more feet to go before reaching the top.

And then it happened. I hooked my fingers around the edge of a shelf of rock above me that I'd thought was secure, only to have it suddenly give way. With a feeling of disbelief, as though everything had gone into slow motion, I lost my balance and dropped into space, followed by a huge chunk of ledge. I heard David scream, "My God, O my God!"

God was Someone else I'd shut out of my life. All my growing years I had attended a strict religious school where the teachers described God as an angry, vengeful Being who would send me to hell for my sins. I didn't like that God, and I'd decided I wanted no part of Him. I'd go it alone, assuming responsibility for my own actions, instead of cowering in fear before some cruel, mythical judge.

And so, even in my present extremity, falling toward death, I did not call on God. But David continued to cry out, not in prayer, but in an agonized, involuntary repetition of the name.

Now occurred in sequence several events so incredible that I find them hard to believe to this day. I had fallen with my face toward the cliff, but now *my body flipped around in midair*, like a cat's, so that I was facing outward. Consequently, when my feet twice touched slight protrusions in the cliff's surface, I was tilted backward, toward the cliff face, instead of being catapulted farther into space. Then my feet landed on a small ledge, barely wide enough for one person, and the *only ledge on that whole cliff between me and the ground.* A few inches to either side, and I would have fallen past it. Sliding *between* two large cacti, I came to a halt with my legs hanging over the ledge. In one more second, I should have been crushed by the falling shelf of rock, which was several cubic feet in size. Instead, just before it would have hit me, it *veered inexplicably to the right,* grazing my shoulder and arm as it roared past.

I hung there in a daze, clutching at my narrow perch with my left hand while watching that boulder fall away toward the canyon floor one hundred fifty feet below. David came scrambling back down the cliff, frantically calling out to me. As he drew near, I heard him breathe, "Thank God, you're alive!" And then his voice changed as he groaned, "Susan— your leg . . ."

As yet, I felt no pain. Consequently, it was with amazement that I viewed my shattered left leg. Through the tattered remnants of my jeans, I saw three holes in the flesh of my lower leg from which broken bones protruded. My foot hung twisted around at an odd angle, like the leg of a discarded doll. I turned my head away, only to see that the inside of my right arm had been sliced completely open, elbow to wrist, exposing ripped ligaments and tendons, and a rubbery length of artery—scratched but not severed—pulsing deep inside the gaping wound.

I looked back toward David and saw that he had turned dead-white. He asked me if I thought my spine was damaged. I took mental inventory of my body, trying to determine if I had internal injuries, but I just couldn't tell. At last David said, "I don't dare try to get you off this cliff alone. I'm going to have to leave you and go for help."

I knew he was right. But the initial shock that had numbed me was beginning to wear off. I was suddenly hit by pain so devastating it froze my breath.

"Hurry—just hurry," I gasped.

He scrambled away at an angle up the ridge, heading toward the mesa and the trail that would take him out of these rugged Sangre de Cristo mountains (a Spanish name meaning 'Blood of Christ') toward the jeep road, far away, where we'd left our four-wheel-drive pickup truck. I knew that the nearest hospital had to be in Española, New Mexico, about twenty miles away. I also knew it would take hours for a rescue crew to hike in with a litter. The light faded fast, taking with it the last heat from the sun. I began to shiver in my thin shirt, for September nights in the high country get very cold. In the distance I heard the rumbling thunder of an approaching storm.

As the minutes passed, the pain grew in intensity until I felt consumed by it. The storm arrived, bringing darkness and an icy rain. The surface of the ledge became slick with water and mud, so that I had to concentrate all my strength in my left arm, trying to hold on.

My mind whirled with giddiness. It would be so easy to let go and slip into that void. To die, and end the pain.

I'd recently read a book called *Life After Life* in which people who had been declared clinically dead returned to life with stories about having met a sentient light filled with love. I didn't know if such a Being existed. But if it did, it couldn't be that hateful personage called "God."

I wanted to pray to that light, but I didn't know what to call it. Finally, I did call it God, for want of a better name. I prayed for help to arrive, and for the strength to hold on until then. I said I was frightened. I said I didn't want to be alone.

And He came.

I saw no light. I heard no voice. All I can tell you is that suddenly, beside me on that ledge, there was a Presence. A Presence filled with warmth and love. I could feel strength pouring into me from that Presence, joining with, and energizing, my own fading will.

The thoughts in my mind were in my own voice, but they said, *Hold on. You can make it. You are not alone. Help will come.*

The comfort I felt in this Presence is indescribable. Whenever I would begin to fade out, something would snap me awake once more and I would discover just enough will-power left in me to pull away from the edge.

But I wanted more. I wanted the touch of a human hand. All these years, I had kept people away. Now, suspended in air on this cold cliff, crying out in pain with almost every breath, I longed desperately for someone to hold me, to talk to me, to distract me from the prison of agony my body had become.

Time flowed into a meaningless blur. And then, between my cries, I heard someone, faint and far away, calling my name. Peering down into the darkness, I saw a tiny light bobbing along the canyon floor.

I called to that light, and the light answered. I saw it veer toward me and proceed, slowly but surely, up the cliff. A face came into view over the side of the ledge, eerily white in the flashlight's glow.

It was a child. A boy about twelve or thirteen years old. I thought for a moment that I was hallucinating. But the boy scrambled up beside me on the slippery ledge. He carefully set the flashlight down in a depression in the rocks. And then he took a folded blanket from his shoulder and draped it over me, shielding me from the rain.

"Who are you?" I whispered.

"I'm Michael," he replied.

He was real. The touch of his small, dirt-roughened hands told me that. He explained that David, frantically looking for a phone, had shown up at the door of Michael's house, outside the canyon. But Mr. Browne, Michael's father, had no phone and was too ill to help with any kind of rescue effort. After hastily telling the Brownes about the accident, David had rushed away, heading once more down the mountain in his search for help.

"I thought you might be cold," Michael said, "so I came to find you."

He said he'd ridden his dirt bike until the brush got too

thick. Then he'd hiked on into the canyon, and at last he'd heard my cries.

He asked what he could do for me, and I suggested that he elevate my injured arm. Surprisingly, my wounds had clotted soon after the accident, so I was no longer bleeding profusely; but elevating the arm seemed to help ease the pain. However, as we shifted on the ledge, I once more slipped toward the edge. Michael quickly grabbed my shoulders and held on, stopping my fall. After he had maneuvered me back to relative safety, he continued to hang on to me, while assuring me that the rescuers would arrive soon. He made me talk in order to keep me awake. Each time I started to slide forward on the slick surface of the ledge, Michael tightened his hold, dragging me back again. He was so determined to save me that I am convinced, had I actually gone over the edge, he would not have released his hold, but would have fallen with me to his own death.

As my mind wandered, I got to thinking that Michael might be a guardian angel. But he chattered on, like any normal boy, telling me about his friends in the Española Junior High and asking me questions just to make sure I was still with him.

I had totally lost track of time. I know now that Michael held me on that ledge for over two hours before more lights appeared in the canyon—David, with a doctor and two paramedics.

The ordeal they went through for the next several hours getting me off the cliff is another story. All I can say is that there were many acts of heroism from them all as they climbed the slippery rocks, splinting my leg and arm, strapping me into a litter, lowering me on ropes to the canyon floor. Michael acted as messenger, relaying instructions from one rescuer to another. All this in cold, wet darkness.

As groggy as I was, I still realized their terrible danger, and my prayer changed: *Please, God, don't let one of them die on this cliff in helping me.*

Because of a head injury I hadn't even known about, the doctor was not able to give me pain-killers. My screams, every time I was accidentally jostled, had to be unnerving for the men, but they didn't give up. Even though they were cold and exhausted, they carried me as carefully as they could over the rough canyon floor and up the slopes to the pickup truck, then drove me over rocky jeep trails to the road where the ambulance waited. Because of the seriousness of my injuries, the doctors in Española couldn't treat me, but sent me on to St. Vincent's Hospital in Santa Fe. At last, twelve hours after my fall, I went into surgery, where the doctors pieced my torn and broken body back together.

I awoke to find myself immobilized in heavy casts. Me, Ms. Independence, totally helpless and having to rely on others for everything—bedpans, baths, food, therapy. Dozens of flower arrangements and over a hundred cards arrived, soon filling my room. Friends and acquaintances flocked to see me, saying eagerly, "You've always been such a loner, Susan, holding us off. But at last we're going to get to do something for you!"

The God I met on that ledge was neither angry nor condemning. The God I met there was love. Love, flowing from an unseen Presence to give me strength; love, coming from David and the rescue team as they struggled to get me off the cliff; love from doctors, nurses, and old friends; and love from Michael, a child who sustained me during that lonely, painful night.

When that rock fell, so did the wall I'd built around myself to shut out that love. I will never be the same.

EASTER AFFIRMATION
Elizabeth Searle Lamb

Today
   the risen Christ
   is risen in my heart
   in radiant, joyous Eastertide.
All doubts,
all fears . . .
   the stone has rolled them all aside
   and faith springs up, alive,
   to welcome Him
today.

THE PROMISE
Debbie Parvin

*I*t was a warm, hazy, Illinois morning, the first of July—I remember waking up tired. Not just a yawn-and-stretch-before-getting-up tired, but a deep-down, aching fatigue.

"I guess I haven't recovered from the recital yet," I told myself, thinking back to a studio dance recital my students had given two weeks earlier. And with three young children home for summer vacation, my choir practice, fellowship group at church . . . well, that was good reason to be a little weary.

I lay back down on the pillow. In college I had always been into everything—dancing, singing, campus choirs, clubs, always racing for some meeting. And now with a family, it was still go, go, go. *It'll always be this way,* I thought.

Reminding myself that I had three children who would be up soon—my husband, Chuck, was already at work—I climbed out of bed . . . and fell flat on my back. *What a klutz!* I thought, as I tried to get up but couldn't. I crawled slowly backward down the stairs to the living room, and hoisted myself onto the sofa.

Surely this won't last, I thought. But it did. The pain grew daily in intensity, sharp and piercing, jumping without any pattern from one part of my body to another. Muscle spasms locked my back in an arched position for hours on end. Finally, I had to be hospitalized.

Meanwhile, a team of doctors worked feverishly to discover what disease I had. Results of test after test were sent to many clinics, and for six agonizing months there was no answer. And then . . . "Dermatomyositis," my doctor told Chuck. "It will slowly destroy Debbie's muscles and vital organs. And we have no cure."

By now I couldn't sit up for more than a half hour at a time. I was too weak to lift a magazine or answer the telephone. As time went on, the doctor's words to my husband held no hope: "She'll be completely bedridden within two years, and probably won't live longer than five years." Period. I was a professional dancer who could no longer walk; a mother who no longer had the strength to raise her five-, seven-, and nine-year-old children.

I might have given up right there, if not for a very strange and wonderful thing that happened during that first hospital stay.

I was alone in my room, half asleep. Some friends from the church had stopped by earlier to visit. Chuck was at work, so I knew he wouldn't be in until later. That's why I was so surprised when I heard those words so distinctly, as if someone were talking to me. I opened my eyes, but there wasn't anyone else in the room—only those words, still ringing in my ears: "The joy of the Lord is your strength."

"Why, I recognize that," I said. "It's from Nehemiah, the tenth verse of the eighth chapter." And then I laughed. I had always believed in God and the Bible, but the one thing I had never been able to do was memorize specific verses, not even as a youngster in Sunday school classes. "The joy of the Lord is your strength. Nehemiah eight, ten." The words came again, clear and unmistakable. I had to find out.

When Chuck came in, I greeted him quickly. "You must read a Bible verse to me. In Nehemiah, chapter eight, verse ten."

Chuck took my Bible off the night stand, flipped the pages to Nehemiah and said, "Well, it says, 'Then he said to them, "Go your way, eat. . . ." ' Why do you want me to read this?"

"Just keep reading. Please."

" ' ". . . and do not be grieved, for the joy of the Lord is your strength." ' That's all there is."

I fought to sit up in bed a little. "Honey, you know I've never been able to memorize Bible verses, right?"

"Yes."

"Today I started repeating that verse, perfectly, in my mind. And I don't remember hearing it before. I think God has given me this verse as His promise, that His strength will always sustain me. This is God's promise that I will be healed."

And so began a journey of faith, buoyed by a verse that had been as unknown to me as the illness that had brought it to me.

After I was released from the hospital, Chuck asked for night duties at the Chicago newspaper where he worked, so he could stay with me during the day while the children were at school. We remodeled the house, putting as much as possible on one floor of our split-level so I could get around in my wheelchair. Friends and neighbors brought meals, did the laundry and housework, offered prayers. I prayed for healing, too—and anticipated a miracle.

Although I was severely restricted, I continued to sing in the church choir for a while. As a form of therapy, my doctor allowed me to continue teaching dance, offering verbal rather than physical instructions. I sometimes taught while lying on a couch in my downstairs studio. I played games with our three children and gave them singing lessons. And all the while I remembered my promise: "The joy of the Lord is your strength."

But a healing, even a respite, didn't come. As weeks turned into months and then into years, I was progressively forced to give up even the simplest outside activities. Although there were days when I might walk fifty steps at one time, it was usually the exception rather than the rule. There was always pain; often hospitalization was the only way to control it. And as my health began to ebb away, so did that kinetic energy of living. The simplest of activities would sap all my strength.

Chuck had become both Dad and Mom, the breadwinner and the breadmaker. By noon, after soothing my anxieties, he was off to the local McDonald's, serving hamburgers to help meet our mounting medical bills. Then home to greet the children after school, before he and they fixed dinner. And after watching a favorite television show with the children and settling them into bed, it was off to be night editor at the *Tribune*.

The children had to adjust too, suddenly faced with responsibility beyond their years. There was no one to catch them in the cookie jar, sure; but there was also no mother to take them to Cub Scouts, to write out an algebra problem, to be waiting up for them after a night out. Usually all I could do was listen to them, and I did, too, every chance I got. I hung on every word of every story they told me, stories that before the illness I was too busy to hear. If I was strong enough to take thirty steps, twenty-seven were for the children—meeting them at the door after school, sharing breakfast. I loved them dearly, and needed them to know that.

I passed the five-year limit the doctor had set, the joy of being alive always tempered by the loneliness and frustration life meant. The only sure element in the uncertainty of disease, in the struggle to keep hope, was Nehemiah—day and night I embraced those words as a small child does a favorite blanket or toy.

Church was my special treat—I insisted on going as often as I was able. "Please, Chuck," I remember pleading after one particularly bad week. "I *have* to be there."

Chuck agreed and, after wheeling me up the special ramp the church had built, helped me to my feet and took my arm in his. Ever so slowly we walked down the center aisle of the First Presbyterian Church in Arlington Heights—step, rest, another step or two. I always tried hard to smile, because it helped me forget the pain. About halfway down and five minutes later, Chuck guided me into a pew, and helped support me during the service. It was a process we were to repeat many times. Together, I hoped, we could persevere.

Eight, nine, ten years passed—children started off to college. Chuck swapped hamburgers for high-school teaching, and I prayed. It was one thing I could do easily. Then, in 1972, eleven years after that dreadful morning, my doctor gave up hope as the disease intensified.

"Debbie, I can't allow you to increase your medication. We've reached the absolute maximum limit. I'm sorry . . ." He paused. "There is nothing more I can do for you."

My muscles were so useless that most days I had difficulty turning over in bed. Chuck wore a brave face, but my insistence that healing would yet come rang hollow against my medical chart.

Then one night in November, as I lay in bed, I was praying. Suddenly I had a sensation of someone else being in the room.

I opened my eyes; and there, not five feet away, He stood—His long, bluish-white robe flowing, His arms outstretched toward me. There were no clearly distinguishable features about Him, only a soft glow. I felt an indescribable blend of shock, amazement, reverence, awe. There was no doubt in my mind that I was seeing Jesus.

"You have been healed," He said in a very audible, very compassionate voice. He went on to tell me certain things. That I was not to stop using the wheelchair and the medication at once, only gradually. That He had given the doctors and researchers their abilities, and that to stop treatment immediately would be a defiance of that gift. Finally He told me not to tell anyone what had happened—not just yet. Then He was gone.

For a moment I just stared, but then, as naturally as taking a breath, I began to stand up. I had been on my knees, at the side of the bed, the entire time. I didn't know how I had gotten there, only that now I was standing. I hadn't been able to do that in ten years.

I walked—that was a miracle in itself—to my dressing room, where my medication was stored. Just as I had been told, I took a slightly reduced amount of my nightly dosage. At that point, I was taking more than three dozen pills a day.

It was difficult not to tell anyone—especially Chuck—but soon my drastic turnaround in health began speaking for itself. "I don't know what's happening," my doctor said during one of my routine examinations. "You were sinking so fast before, and now you seem to be getting better. I've never known of anyone with your disease to have a remission like this."

I felt the time had come. "Thanks to your efforts," I began cautiously, "and to God's healing power, it isn't a remission. I just don't have it anymore."

His look was incredulous. "Debbie, I don't believe that, and I can't accept it. I'm afraid this good spell is only temporary."

But future test results only affirmed my faith—there was no sign of dermatomyositis anywhere in my body. And my heart, damaged by the disease, now was perfect; an ulcer and hernia were also healed.

Just as Jesus had said that night, it took me more than a year and a half to free myself completely from the wheelchair and medication. But since that time—for more than six years now—I have been free of the disease.

Was my meeting with Jesus just a dream, my healing a remission? Some still choose to believe that, and that is their choice. But the fact remains that once I was crippled, now I am whole. Once I couldn't walk, but now, by the grace of God, I can dance.

It was a long and difficult wait, thirteen years of pain and grief. I don't know why God chose to heal me when He did. But I do know that until He did, He sustained me and those around me with the strength and patience we needed to cope with those days and years of pain. And He still does today.

Truly, the joy of the Lord is my strength. In sickness and in health.

THE PAINTING
Bill Zdinak

I guess I was what you might call a lost soul—or something very close to it—when the telephone call came. It was from a member of the Bridgeport (Connecticut) Congregational Church, and I remember how bored and impatient I felt as I listened to her. She knew that I was an artist, she said. She wanted to know if I would submit a painting for the church's annual art show, five months away.

In those days I took the line of least resistance about almost everything. If the show was almost half a year away, I figured I could worry about it later. In any case, it was easier to say yes than to say no. "Oh, sure," I told her. "I'll submit something." And hung up. And promptly forgot all about it.

One reason I wasn't interested in the church member's call was that there was no money in it and, as usual, I was looking for the big deal. Two years earlier, in 1960, what seemed like a very big deal had been right in my hands, and then had slipped through my fingers as the result of an incredible freak accident that almost took my life.

The deal had been a contract with a major automobile manufacturer to help promote a new car. It was all signed, and a lot of money was involved. To celebrate, I had agreed to go with some friends on a fishing trip to Canada. One morning, after a walk around the lake, I came back ready for a shower. Forgetting the warnings I'd had that the water was very hot, I stepped into the enclosed tub and shut the glass doors. In minutes the water turned to scalding steam. The glass door was stuck, and I couldn't slide it open. The pain was terrible. I began screaming at the top of my lungs. I couldn't reach forward to the handle on the water. My legs became numb, I couldn't see, and I had a terrifying fear that I would be blinded! That would mean the end of my career!

I started to fall, and my hand went through the glass. Suddenly I knew I had to hurl myself through the door to escape from that scalding prison. I covered my eyes and somersaulted through the glass. My head hit the opposite wall and I lay on the bathroom floor in a jumbled mass of shattered glass and blood.

My friends finally managed to get a doctor, who spent more than two hours stitching up my wounds. My life was saved, but during my period of recuperation, I discovered that

I couldn't draw any more. I had lost the use of my hands. The automobile manufacturer's project fell through. All my hopes and dreams had gone down the drain.

For anyone else, this experience might have been the time for some soul-searching and for a real reevaluation of goals and values, but I viewed my experience at that time only as a humiliating defeat. I felt that God had let me down, and I was bitter and resentful.

I found work as a consultant and was able to support my family, but I still measured success only in terms of money. That was unfortunate because, materially speaking, things went from bad to worse. Finally I lost my own studio, and a large New York firm offered to back me in a small shop. I wasn't particularly concerned about the integrity of the firm, and it turned out that they were dishonest. I was lucky to get out with only a minimal loss.

So here I was, back where I had started—still trying to make a lot of money fast, and still bombing. After two years, I regained about 75 percent use of my hands and was able to draw again, but things just didn't pick up for me. None of my deals panned out. I kept brooding about the lost contract and wondering why my life had got into such a mess. It was about that time I got the call from the Bridgeport Congregational Church.

Five months can go by very quickly. One day the phone rang, and I heard a vaguely familiar voice saying, "Mr. Zdinak, we don't have your painting yet—the one for our annual exhibit."

I remembered then, all right.

In my usual manner I had promised everything and fulfilled nothing. But even now a lie was easier than the truth. "I'm sorry," I said. "I don't have it quite finished yet." I was really disgusted with myself. Why hadn't I just told her I had forgotten it?

She asked me what size it was. Glancing around the room, I saw a frame with my wife's picture in it. So I gave her that size. "Fine," she said, "we'll save that space for you. But we really need it soon. Please don't let us down!"

I started then to contrive a religious picture. But nothing worked. By 2:00 A.M., twelve hours later, I had made a dozen worthless starts. Angry thoughts raged through my head. *I'm a phony and I'm so sick of living this way. My life is a mess. Everything is a mess. I can't make it on my own.* In complete frustration I cried out, "O God! This is what I get for lying! Please help me."

I threw down my brushes, and instantly there was a flash of light in the room. In that split second I saw on the canvas the image I was to paint. It was a head of Christ, but it was to be composed of many small faces—men, women and children of all races and backgrounds, national and spiritual leaders as well as ordinary people. *That's it!* I thought, and hastily grabbed pictures of faces from around the studio. I began to paint in a way I had never known before. I did each face with rapid brush strokes and no preliminary sketches. Some unseen power guided my hand; I couldn't seem to make a false stroke. I knew something wonderful was happening, and I thought, *God, just let it continue.*

In fifteen hours all the faces had been finished. I stepped back to view the work and knew that it was the best thing I had ever done. Artists and art critics told me later that it was impossible for me to have done such a painting so quickly. I don't really understand what happened, but I do know that the painting is the best thing that ever happened in my life.

Over the years, it has continued to work its positive effect. Art shows continue to exhibit it. In each show it attracts crowds of viewers. People who have seen it tell me they've found it spiritually uplifting; in some cases it has inspired people to the extent that their lives have been changed.

I have refused to accept any profits from the painting because it isn't really my doing any more than my life is any longer my own life. It taught me an important lesson. Every time in the past when I tried to play all the angles and make the big money, something went wrong. Now my life is a success, and I give all the credit where it belongs—to God.

I have become deeply committed to working for Christ. Christ is in my life every day, not just on Sunday. I turn down advertising work if I feel it is selling something I can't morally approve. I try to accept only work that is pleasing to God. I begin my day and end my day thanking Him. I never knew what success really meant until I gave myself up to Him and let Him be my guide. I find that He is with me just as He promised—always—and everywhere.

His Mysterious Ways, Volume III, was created by the same people who publish *Guideposts*, a monthly magazine filled with true stories of people's adventures in faith. If you have enjoyed this book, we think you'll find help and inspiration in the exciting stories that appear in our magazine. *Guideposts* is not sold on the newstand. It's available by subscription only. And subscribing is easy. All you have to do is write

Guideposts Associates, Inc.,
39 Seminary Hill Road
Carmel, New York, 10512.

For those with special reading needs, *Guideposts* is published in Big Print, Braille, and Talking Magazine.